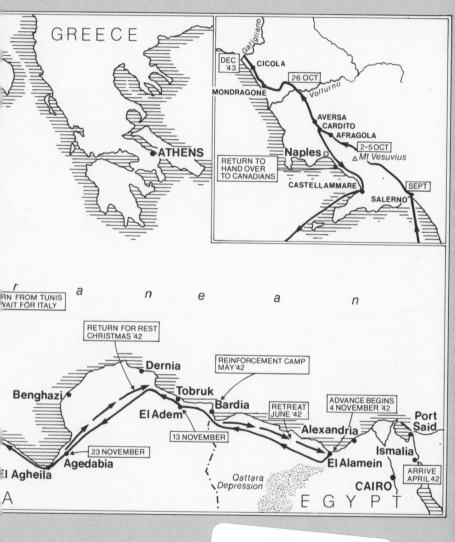

North Africa and Italy 1942–43.

To the Mackenzies.

THE 8.15 TO WAR

with Best Wishes
Peter Roach
Christmas '82

With lots of love
from Sal xxx.

THE 8.15 TO WAR

Memoirs of a Desert Rat

*El Alamein, Wadi Halfa, Tunis, Salerno,
Garigliano, Normandy and Holland*

PETER ROACH

Leo Cooper in Association with
Secker & Warburg

First published in 1982
by Leo Cooper in association with
Martin Secker & Warburg Limited
54 Poland Street, London W1V 3DS

ISBN 0 436 41700 6

Photoset, printed and bound in Great Britain by
Redwood Burn Limited, Trowbridge, Wiltshire

This book is dedicated to
The 1st Royal Tank Regiment.

Foreword

by Field Marshal Lord Carver, GCB, CBE, DSO, MC

Peter Roach's description of what he calls the experiences of an ordinary man in war makes nostalgic reading for those who shared some of those experiences with him; but it also provides a truthful, moving and revealing record of the feelings of a man of sensitive imagination both as a merchant seaman in the Battle of the Atlantic and as a soldier of the Royal Armoured Corps in North Africa, Italy and north west Europe in the Second World War. There are no heroics here and no exaggeration; but nothing is left out or glossed over either. This is what war was like.

Preface

This is an effort to write down simply how one very ordinary man felt when involved in the fighting of a war. As wars are now fought by the ordinary man, and as this is one aspect of warfare rarely chronicled, I felt it worth doing. I have tried to be strictly truthful and at the same time to be generous to those I did not understand.

PR.

Chapter 1

As THE FLEET steamed down channel to take up station during the Munich crisis, they passed a tight little sailing ship beating up into soundings. Bound home after two years of wandering; wandering without engines or radio into the odd corners that still existed in 1938. On board, now 21 years old, I had stars in my eyes and a body as dark and hard as the pickled rock elm of the ship's hull.

When next September came again the fleet sailed down channel, not to return for the six grinding years of war. I still had stars in my eyes—which had queried my studies at university and queried the validity of war. I took the easy way out and went back to sea in the Merchant Service.

As a purely civilian service I found myself a ship in London and sailed in the *Castilian* on a three-month voyage down the Mediterranean, returning deep laden with Cyprus oranges just before Christmas. By 1 January I had signed as seaman on the *Anthea*, a dreadful old wreck of a ship, bound for Halifax in Canada. With no cargo or ballast we took twenty-seven days outward bound, were alongside loading grain for twenty hours, and then set off home in convoy.

So passed the period of the phoney war. There was fighting on land and sea and in the air, but as yet rather minor and restrained except for Finland's incredible efforts against the Russians. Merchant ships were sunk with regularity by mine, bomb and torpedo and it became more and more common to sail with men who had been picked up from the sea. However, being away from the wireless and the newspapers we were not aware of what went on, except in our own small world.

Ten days after leaving the *Anthea* I signed to join the *Briarwood*, a small ship and old, but so very different. This time I didn't sign completely blind, for I met the skipper and liked him and his outlook. I walked down the quay to join her and saw a small, well-decked ship with a kink in her bow: heritage of an accident while docking in Canada the summer before. Some cement had reinforced any weakness and there was no longer time to repair eyesores.

On board I found things very different from the two previous ships. Perhaps most important was an air of order and control, the outcome of good officers and a wonderful bos'n. Allied to this was the fact that the ship was looked after as well as the exigencies of war would allow. It was only necessary to look at the crew's quarters to realise that the owners of this ship had their own ideas.

The crew's quarters were aft as they had been on the *Castilian*, but here any similarity ended. We were berthed three to a cabin, each man with his own wardrobe and drawers, the straw mattress replaced with foam rubber. There was linoleum on the floor, a central stove for heating the radiators, a small drying cupboard, mess room—bare but pleasant—and a magnificent bathroom with terrazo flooring and a real bath. Unfortunately all water was still midships.

The *Briarwood* hailed from the north-east and quite a few of the crew came from the Shetland isles, making the Tyne their headquarters. I found them some of the nicest people I have ever sailed with. This included the bos'n, a man of huge size and immense knowledge and dignity, who kept us busy, but happy and proud of our

2

work. Also there was a young Australian who was working for his second mate's ticket—a promising fruit until I met the maggot. An unfortunate man of some education, who had held a mate's ticket and lost it through drink, now further down the road to alcoholism he was bitter and carping and liked to collect around him a group of accolytes who would groan in unison with him over his imagined grievances.

We sailed from London for Swansea to load anthracite and used the voyage round to shake down. Like the *Castilian* we had regular gun drills under an ex-marine, but besides the four-inch naval gun we had a twelve-pound high-angle gun for aircraft defence. We had little faith in either ourselves or our weapons, but they made a show.

We docked late in Swansea and were hoping to get ashore before the pubs shut when the bos'n intimated that there was overtime to be worked. As the rate for the job was 10 pence an hour we were not very happy. I was just about to burst forth on the iniquities of life when a vast kindly hand dropped on my shoulder and the bos'n suggested that we get on with it. We did.

The next few days were full of dust as the coal was tipped into the holds, and we and everything we had became filthy. To add to our annoyance the trimmers, whose job it was to shovel the coal down into the corners, spent much of their time playing cards by candlelight in those very corners, thus delaying the day when we might clear up the mess.

We sailed on the night tide, so that it was dark when the tugs came alongside and made off with our heavy wire cables while we tried desperately to make them fast round the bollards. Digger and I, working at the stern, found ourselves in a desperate slanging match with the tug skipper, which was finally resolved when he ran into the quay while mouthing oaths at us and our fathers.

The sun shone and by diligent use of the hose and days of scrubbing our quarters, we reduced the ship to a proper state of cleanliness. On our own we blithely made our way across to Boston to arrive the day the *Blitzkrieg* broke over Europe. In spite of the warm sun and the sight of pretty girls in summer dresses crossing the bridge nearby, this was not a very happy time. The newspapers carried banner headlines of one disaster after another, so that to keep a calm face in an alien land was not easy.

Fortunately I got away for a weekend and went down to New York to stay with a friend and was filled with music and talk and things hopeful and academic. It seemed odd to be talking to my own kind who could plan what they would do next; I hadn't realised how we had all forfeited our freedom of action once war started.

Empty of our coal and with a solid foundation of steel bars in the bottom of the holds we headed north around Nova Scotia, making our way to Newcastle in New Brunswick. As so often seems to happen in the world of ships, we arrived with the grey light of day when the water and low coastline looked bleak and unfriendly. A small motor launch came out bringing the pilot, a lean weatherbitten man of no pretensions with the strong features of a bluenose fisherman.

Incredibly we wound our way up river, past fields bright green with grass and graced by elegant dairy cows. Farmsteads stood neat and ordered under the clear bright light of early day. This was an idyllic rural scene, so peaceful and so far removed from the normal port areas.

Newcastle seemed hardly more than a large village and we tied up to the jetty beside the road; rather we parked beside the road. However, there was nothing sleepy or antiquated about the loading of our pit props and we enjoyed the friendliness and hospitality of the people. But overlaying all was the constant news from Europe, which grew grimmer and grimmer and though our heads may have been high our hearts were heavy. Digger and I went, on the last evening, to a small café and ate a superlative meal of grilled salmon and strawberry shortcake.

Soon loaded we prepared to make our way back to Halifax to load a deck cargo as well. This we could not do here because the bar at the river mouth was too shallow. As we crossed the bar we just touched the bottom and a quiver ran through the ship, but no more.

We sailed in convoy from Halifax with the well decks so piled high with pit props that we had to make our way across the top of them when going from our quarters to the midship section. At least it gave us vast extra buoyancy in case of need. The weather and the enemy were kind and we received no news bulletins. It was not long before we were making our way calmly up the Channel under a hot blue sky. Ahead of us and moving at right angles was a small coasting vessel; standing on the fore deck were a lot of soldiers. We waved in a friendly way but they only stood and looked dejected.

We anchored off the downs. Word had got around that things were not well and we clustered round a small radio in the firemen's mess and listened to Winston Churchill telling of the fall of France and how the British were alone. Immediately there was a horrified silence. A large fireman with a florid face and no front teeth sat heavily down. 'The end' he said. And then we revived and heads came up. I produced the days of Nelson, when similarly we had been alone. Slowly the sore dispersed and vows were secretly made. There was a purpose greater than any of us and from this minute the crew became one. No longer were we sailors, fireman and catering staff, no longer men and officers, but there was a unity. Each needed the other and Britain needed the cargoes. From the little donkey man who came to sea with a cardboard box full of clay pipes to the vast calm bos'n with a twinkle in his eye and a wisdom of the world uncluttered by formal learning, we all knew that we were part of the whole.

We made our way north up the North Sea, a sea still and hazy under a hot sun. Overhead was the drone of planes. Mine-sweepers were busy clearing the sea lanes—a sharp rattle of machine gun fire and an explosion as they removed the hazard of a floating mine.

In Sunderland the dockers seemed more dilatory than ever and we chafed at the slowness of our unloading. Our nights were no longer free for during air-raids we must man the anti-aircraft gun. From Sunderland we went empty round to the Tyne where our degaussing gear was repaired and renewed and then, remarkably short of sleep, we sailed away south. On board we had some soldiers with machine guns as protection against low-flying aircraft. Fortunately we had no need of them, but I did manage to buy a magnificent duffel coat from one of them for a few shillings. A souvenir, he told me, from Narvik and the battles in the north of Norway.

Off Spurn Head urgent messages were sent ordering us into Hull. The apocryphal story was that, because our engine room staff, 'blacksmiths' we called them, had connected the wiring up the wrong way round, the degaussing gear, instead of removing the magnetic effect of the steel hull, had actually turned the ship into a floating electromagnet. Whether this was true or no, we had three days of respite which we enjoyed. I bought a typewriter and spent the next year writing a book about a beloved sailing ship and the vast tranquillity of the Pacific.

Outward bound again to join a convoy in the Thames estuary. In my pocket I had a letter from my father giving me an address in Canada to which I could go

6

should Britain have fallen by the time we came to return. Such were our thoughts as we tried to go competently about our business.

With our sisters in the convoy we wound our way through the minefields bound for the Channel. Now there were rows of masts to guide the way, standing calmly clear of the devouring water. As we steamed past Dover we could hear the wail of air-raid sirens and a plane swooping down from over the land dropped a stick of bombs across our path. They fell wide but covered us with spray as we worked on the fore deck. This was war as it should be: sudden, safe and exhilarating.

Coming clear of the land we formed into four lines and set off, zigzagging down channel under the paternal eye of our escort, a mine-sweeping trawler with a double Lewis gun. Hearts were light in the wonderful weather and these waters were seldom troubled by U-boats.

When I went to the wheel in the early afternoon of the following day the four columns of ships were marching serenely on down the blue Channel. In the middle the trawler bobbed and curtsied quietly while overhead droned a solitary Anson. Above and behind us, skittishly in the warm summer air, flew our large white kite—a hazard to dive bombers. Away on the port side, but quite clear, was the French coast. We remarked this quietly but made no comment.

I stood at the wheel, gently correcting the *Briarwood* as she strayed from her course. Ahead through the narrow aperture I could see the trawler and two ships, while through the glass panel in the port side door I caught glimpses of a small Norwegian coaster deep laden and happy with the gentleness of the sea. My lunch settled quietly and I considered chapter two of the book which was already on the typewriter.

Then all over the convoy I could hear klaxons grating. Swift feet rang on the bridge ladder, orders were shouted. I heard the noise of planes and suddenly the racket of machine guns, the dull thump of bombs and the staccato bang of anti-aircraft guns. Through the port door I saw a large cloud of black smoke in place of the coaster, but beneath it nothing. My head seemed very near the deckhead above me. I took one hand from the wheel and held my thigh above the knee to stop it shivering.

Outside on the bridge I heard the captain and third mate. At intervals they dived for shelter. I heard our twelve-pounder banging. There I stood, alone and immobile, knowing what I must do. I must stand there quietly keeping the *Briarwood* on a steady course. I must require no comfort or guidance, leaving the officers free to their tasks. I stood in my cell, unable to see what went on, a very frightened little man steering quietly down channel.

And then it was all finished, as all terrible things must eventually finish, and the third mate came back into the wheelhouse. We both found a blessed relief from the tension in talking. I was given a profit and loss account, though it seemed mainly loss; our gun crew made claims to having damaged a plane, but that was the total profit. The skipper was busy picking bullets out of the sandbagging on the bridge and holding them aloft as if they had been especially aimed at him.

My relief came and I stepped thankfully out into the fresh air and made my way aft to the gun platform to take my place as a supply number on the twelve-pounder. This was better; here were fellow humans for comfort, here was some sort of action and here it was possible to see, and if need be to move. As the convoy steamed quietly away from the French coast my fellows pointed out the gaps left by the raid. The trawler marched defiantly in the middle; the Anson had presumably and wisely gone.

Some time later they returned. Away astern and high in the air like a swarm of mosquitos on a still evening, they drew near and it all started again; but this time there wasn't the same fear. We watched the attack pressed home on other ships with compassion. When our turn came we were busy on the gun. Here we were really lucky for the great majority of the ships had no sort of offensive weapon against aircraft and must just steam slowly on and hope.

A Stuka dive bomber came rocketing down on us from astern and met the kite skirmishing in its path. We started firing and it withdrew with smoking exhausts. To starboard a ship was hit and turned out of control and rammed its neighbour. On we steamed, leaving the halt and the maim. Evening came and then the darkness of night and now it was the turn of the E-boat.

And those that were left came into Plymouth.

Time is a wonderful healer and fear tissue forms fast. By the end of the first day at anchor we were constantly one of the first ships with a gun cleared when the sirens sounded. How much easier it is to be aggressive than to be passive. We sailed round the coast for Milford Haven and joined another convoy.

Once more we set out. Off the south of Ireland we broke down and as we rolled gently on the long blue swells the convoy drew remorselessly away and we were alone. For twenty-four hours wearily we pitched and rolled, while the engine room staff worked furiously with boiler tubes. Voices were hushed, no longer did steel doors clang and boots ring on the steel decks but an anxious quiet lay over the ship. As darkness fell we went quietly about our duties and no glimmer of light showed in the night.

After twenty-four hours the engines started again and

I lay in my bunk listening with pleasure to the thrash of the screw, 'hurry, hurry, hurry', and felt the quiver of the plates as the engines pulsed. So on our own and feeling vulnerable in this vast expanse of sea and sky we fled westwards. Twice we sighted other ships making off furtively in divergent directions. The pressure was now beginning to be felt; with the Atlantic ports of France at their disposal the U-boats could roam freely and were helped by long-range aircraft using French airfields.

The normal hazards of storm and fire, collision and illness, accident and wrecking, to these now were added mines: plain, acoustic or magnetic. Attack by submarine with torpedo or gunfire, attack from the air, and attack from surface ship. Travelling in convoy increased the hazards of collision enormously—although not likely on a bright sunny day with ships at respectful distance from each other, good visability and the joy of a warm back. Even then a breakdown in the steering gear could slew a ship across the path of the oncoming convoy, across ships ponderous to manoeuvre, with no brakes, no accelerator and vast momentum. But on a black night, with all ships closed up and only a tiny glimmer of light to follow, it was hazardous indeed. Once at the wheel in these circumstances the gyro compass died and I stood helpless, holding the wheel amidships. Completely blind, we couldn't stop for fear of ships driving up from the rear. Whatever happened we mustn't show a light. Were we veering to the left or right? Were we still in line? Out of the howling night loomed the stern quarters of a ship and we knew temporarily where we were.

Fog was a constant hazard off the Newfoundland banks. Once we sailed from Halifax out to sea wrapped in a warm wet blanket and hardly saw a ship for the first three days, but followed the hooting of the leader of our line, while around us we could hear the mournful wail of

10

the other lines and the occasional threshing of screws. At least in these conditions we were free from attack.

Slowly but surely the pressures increased; everyone knew of sunken ships, had seen them sunk, had been sunk by bomb, mine or torpedo. In 1940 Geordie made an eight-week voyage to Portugal. The ship went ashore in a gale near Porto but the crew were saved. Coming home on another ship they were bombed and sunk and picked up; two hours later they were torpedoed and sunk. A fourth ship brought Geordie home.

Ore-carrying ships sunk like stones; tankers blew up or blazed in the centre of a burning sea or, perhaps worse, filled the lungs of the struggling swimmers with thick black oil. Ammunition ships went bang. Engine room staff were trapped below or injured by explosion or scalding steam; sleeping men were trapped in their bunks or mortally injured were they lay; men died of bitter cold and exposure on open rafts; gaunt famished men went mad from lack of water in sun-bleached boats.

All this we knew—and it weighed with us. The sudden sharp bang as a following sea struck the counter brought figures suddenly upright in their bunks, only slowly to lie back again. The playful dolphin streaking towards the joy of a tumbling bow wave left a long phosphorescent streak, a torpedo until it turned aside with a loop of joy. The thud as a torpedo struck an unfortunate sister. The glow astern sinking lower on the horizon while the convoy went on, on. We knew it was the cargoes that mattered.

Ceaselessly the escorts worked: shepherding, guarding, cajoling. Tiny ships, standing on their noses, rolling sickeningly; never enough of them, over-stretched; yet they generally found time to pick up survivors.

And the men: old and young, phlegmatic or fearful. This was no military force; there were no medical

11

examinations, no age limits and no training for survival. Charlie, the dog snatcher, was 72 and had two teeth; young Charlie was 16. They were a cross-section of the country and they sat on these temporary floating homes and hoped to arrive. This was their job and this they would do.

Under these conditions I found writing a great relief. For an hour or two each day I could forget myself and my surroundings and go back to masts and sails, to deep blue seas and idyllic islands, to a life that promised a to-morrow.

It was at this time that I fell foul of the alcoholic who shared a cabin with Digger and myself. Working on the winches one day he made some cutting remark to the world in general as the bos'n walked by. This was his habit and up till now we had taken no notice for the sake of peace. Perhaps it was the tension under which we now lived or perhaps his remark was more beastly than usual, but the bos'n went scarlet in the face and rasping that he had had enough he picked up the unfortunate man in his vast arms and threw him away contemptuously. No physical damage resulted, apart from some bruises and abrasions, and the bos'n was thereafter left in peace. Instead the odium seemed to have settled on me because I had witnessed the humiliation. Thereafter I became the recipient of snide remarks made to the world in general. I suffered this for some weeks until one night in Newfoundland I met him in the street and when he started the inevitable diatribe I hit him hard in the mouth. From then on when I came into the cabin he went out; when I came into the mess room he went out. I was sorry for him because he was no longer rational, but I could find no common ground on which to approach him. Fortunately he left at the end of the voyage.

So we made our solitary way across to Halifax without incident and from there we were sent to

Cornerbrook in Newfoundland to load pit props, up through the fiords to this small town lying amidst the forests, which supplies so much of the paper for our daily press. Cut off from the sea during the winter when the freeze came, to us this was a frontier town with mainly dirt roads and wooden houses, and a wonderful smell of pine. Here we saw huskies and met people who talked casually about sledges and snow shoes.

The sun shone and we relaxed for a while, ably assisted by the girls of the town who were gay and amorous. In the balmy nights we danced or drank, picnicked or loved; and it was under these gentle emotional conditions that I realised what the war meant to me. Lying out under a waning moon with a breast to lay my head on I choked at the thought of what inevitably lay ahead and when I awoke my heart was harder and my resolve established. I didn't know that I wanted to fight, but I realised that I had got mixed up in a fight and the chances were that I should get hurt. In that case, by temperament, I must join in.

Sadly we said goodbye and made away down the fiord and around to a small fishing village where they towed out rafts of timber and loaded them from out of the water. This in fact was far more of a frontier settlement. Here they talked about floating the sawn timber across the water to build themselves a house. Here they might shoot a moose at the beginning of winter and store it in an ice house to supply meat for a family. Here the fish seemed unlimited and the priest objected to anything as daring as dancing with a member of the opposite sex in your arms; square dancing was the order of the day. We were sad to go.

With the decks piled high with slippery pit props we made our way back to Halifax for a convoy and home. Once more we made our way down the harbour in line ahead and then formed up into lines. We leant on the rails in our spare moments and discussed the ships around us. This was a sort of club; the slow Atlantic convoy. We got to know the ships during successive voyages and we got to know their idiosyncracies. This one was always lagging behind, that one was always making excessive smoke, another strayed from line. We would miss an old acquaintance and then in some dockside pub we would learn of her sinking.

Convoys were now making well up into the north to the short winter days and the rough seas, and also to be as far from the Biscay ports as possible. Up here we saw the aurora borealis flickering across the sky and one night the wireless aerial glowed like a thick golden strand with St Elmo's fire. Lifeboats and rafts were sighted and inspected by the escorts; depth charges sent a thump against the hull of the ship and stirred the sleeping forms. As we came nearer home, aircraft appeared to guard us on our way. Again north about and again to the Tyne. 'Turn around, turn around' was the cry. I managed a weekend at home, but the food which we had bought out in Canada for our families we were not allowed to bring ashore unless we had an import licence. One irate seaman walked to the side with a large ham and threw it in the dock. The rest of us were more restrained and merely kept it on board until we should return again.

Again we went north through the Pentland Firth and down the west coast to Loch Ewe where we awaited a convoy and our slow crawl west across the grey, hungry Atlantic. Once more we rolled and plunged our way westwards, going north up to Iceland where the grey wastes were hidden by the long dark nights. And so we came to the St Lawrence and up to Quebec and a cargo of grain. Winter was approaching and we found the Canadians anything but friendly. In Halifax they merely handed out white feathers, but up here in Quebec the

Canadian army made life so unpleasant that we didn't really bother to go ashore.

With the start of the cold weather we made our way back to Halifax and a deck cargo of timber, and once more out into the Atlantic. We were a big convoy and for the first time we had a large merchant cruiser, the *Jervis Bay*, amongst the escort. I was amused to see the *Castilian* astern of us in the next line. A far cry this from the balmy Mediterranean and loading fruit and wine around the Aegean. A few days out we were joined by some fine ships coming up from the south. Making an imposing sight, this mass of ships steamed steadily eastwards. Cargo boats with undefined goods, tankers, refrigerated ships, ships with aircraft on deck, ships with vehicles on deck, ships stacked with timber, all in line, all in order. And around them the sheep dogs worrying the stragglers, chasing hither and yon, listening, searching, probing for our defence.

I had made a habit of sleeping in pyjamas in the safer areas, but once I thought that we were approaching the danger zone, like the rest of the crew, I slept all standing. I was the sole arbiter of these boundaries, which were constantly moving westwards. I decided that that night, 5 November, was the last safe night, so when I came off watch at 4 p.m. I brought with me a bucket of hot water and repaired to the glory of our bathroom to bath in luxury. I was fit and well and my book was finished and wrapped safely in my life jacket, along with a plug of tobacco and a small bottle of rum. Only the first chapter was missing, which I was rewriting.

Soothed by my wellbeing and the luxury of hot water, I sang hideously and wondered at the incredible joy of just living. At half past five we were sitting around the messroom table about to spoon large portions of Lancashire hot-pot on to our plates when there was the sound of explosions. Geordie, who was nearest, got up

15

and looked out of the porthole. 'They're landing in the convoy' he shouted, and we ran for the deck as the klaxon blared.

Way out on the port beam, barely discernible in the failing light, was a sinister grey shape suddenly lit by the hard yellow flash of its guns. One half of me noticed our ginger cat, belly down, snaking along the top of the timber towards the safety of the fo'c'sle. How did a cat recognise that the danger was real? We had the four-inch gun stripped and ready and then we stood and waited.

Initially the raider fired at a large refrigerated ship of the New Zealand line and the shots were passing over us. The *Jervis Bay* steaming in the centre of the convoy began to turn towards the enemy and they shifted their fire towards her. Astern a Swedish motor ship was signalling frantically with a Morse lamp; to us she was rather like a school fellow trying to get out of a beating by saying that he had been persuaded against his better judgement.

Hardly had the *Jervis Bay* turned than she was hit and fire broke out. As the convoy split up and fled fanwise to the east and south, dropping smoke floats as they went, they watched this flaming torch still steaming against the adversary, still firing while we, perforce, must flee. The *Castilian*, which had always been a laggard in convoys, steamed past us, making nothing less than twelve knots. The grey shape was dead astern of us now and we fired one round at maximum elevation, but were hopelessly out of range. All was grey in the fading light, apart from a great torch of light. I stood on the gun platform and prayed, not for mercy or my salvation, but because faced with possible oblivion it was the natural course.

We went below to collect warm clothes and I took the opportunity to tuck the first chapter of my book into my life jacket. On the mess room table the Lancashire hotpot

16

was congealed; there was no sign of the cat. Darkness fell as we stood grouped around the gun and watched the fight from the flashes. All that remained of the *Jervis Bay* was a saucer of flame low on the horizon, but still there came the great gushes of flame from the guns of the raider, answered now by the little flash of a four-inch gun on some merchant vessel. Another great flash and then a shower of flame and sparks welling into yet another fire glowing in the dark. We felt very humble as we watched. As each cargo ship was singled out for attack it answered as best it could before being reduced to a shambles of flame hissing in the mounting water. A tanker was hit and went up in a great sheet of flame. Still we fled. The wind got up and the sea began to rise and our thoughts turned to those struggling out there in the middle of this vast ocean. The firing became less and less frequent and by midnight we had reverted to normal watches. We were quiet and subdued, for we had seen men die for us.

Alone we made our way eastwards, until some days later when we met up with others of our convoy and were shepherded gently to the Clyde. North about again and down the east coast to discharge at Immingham. And we got a few days' leave on the strength of it. I made my way along the miles of quayside, lugging a suitcase which contained a 56-pound bag of sugar and a lot of tea, which I had tried to bring ashore the voyage before. An obliging policeman helped me carry the case.

Returning to the ship one dark wild night I put my foot under a hose which had been left connected to a vessel and went headlong into the dock. Some eight feet down I met the water and found it remarkably warm. While those on the quay were genuinely concerned lest they had seen the last of me and made off for help, I floated gently in the black dark and searched about for a book which I had been carrying. I was wearing a thick leather jacket zipped down the front and tight at the wrists and waist; this was full of trapped air and kept me floating gently on the surface. When I got back to the ship, apart from my wrists and collar I was quite dry from the waist upwards.

With the ship empty we sailed for the Tyne and up to Jarrow to load coke. This scruffy area, where years before the Venerable Bede had lived and written in tranquillity, received us with its natural warmth and kindness. Lying out in the river the watchman had to use a boat to fetch and carry the crew to the shore. As the Tyne boats have only one oar, I learned to scull over the stern, an ability I have rejoiced in.

When we sailed we were carrying 500 tons of rubble on deck as ballast, which was easily moved on arrival or shovelled over the side when nearly across the Atlantic. All was grey, bleak and cold as we went around the north of Scotland and spent Christmas Day at anchor in Loch Ewe. Ships lay straining at their anchors; work boats drove through the stinging spray; and away to the east were a cluster of buildings lying beneath the low hills. We drank some whisky and the cook did his best, but it only accentuated our position. Far better to forget and live from one day to the next.

Up into the cold and dark, up to the harshness and ferocity of these northern waters in the depths of winter. We passed within sight of Iceland and dropped some ships off there. And then slowly on again until the convoy broke up and it was each ship for itself.

I had equipped myself fairly well for this very cold weather, with my fine duffel coat, a thick leather jacket and the usual warm trousers, shirts and sweaters, but most of the men I sailed with made do with odds and ends of clothing and suffered from their neglect. But this was their trait; today is the day, tomorrow may never come.

Some days out from Boston we set to work to shovel our ballast over the side to save time in our turn round, but we were frustrated by a tearing gale out of the west that brought us into port coated thick with ice from masthead to the water line. Removing the tarpaulin and hatch covers was a slow and agonising task.

The quays were thick with snow when we tied up alongside, but within a very short space of time the first of our cargo of timber was being lowered into the hold. For our part we painted the hull of the ship and painted it very fast, for the only way to keep warm sitting on a plank over the icy waters of the harbour was to keep the paint brush moving.

Again I had a weekend in New York and came back partly refreshed to find the ship nearly loaded. The Americans were very kind to us and we found this strange and unexpectedly pleasant after our experiences in Canada.

With our decks piled high with vast timbers we came up to Halifax and lay in the basin awaiting convoy. I always enjoyed lying at anchor here, not only because of the beauty of the place but because of warm memories of sailing under a hot summer sun when ships could come and go freely and men had a future. This time the surface of the water was thickening with ice and your breath was a mist before your eyes.

Homeward bound we passed close to Iceland again. With half a gale blowing and the water beginning to freeze we were washing the paintwork on the after deck. Eventually even the bos'n relented and we took our frozen hands below. Steadily the gale built up until the convoy broke up, with each ship fighting for itself. By midnight, with heavy seas breaking over the decks, the deck cargo began to move. The watch on deck, who were in the midship section, stayed on duty while we lay dozing on our bunks and listening to the water sloshing through our quarters. To venture across the shifting timber in the dark would have been foolhardy.

Over the radio came a call for help from a ship broken down and with smashed steering gear. With the day the sea began to abate a little and we set to on deck to repair what we could of the damage. A lifeboat was dangling in the sea from one davit and smashing against the side as we rolled. This was our first call and then we must refasten the shambling mess of timber.

Once more the spreadeagled convoy came together. Nearly home now with a great sea running in from abeam and a bright sun, each ship lifting and surging with the rolling waves. I stood at the wheel, one eye on the compass, one eye on the men working on the fore deck lashing down the timber again. Whenever a particularly nasty wave came running towards the bow I let the *Briarwood's* bent nose fall off a little, trying to make sure no sea broke over the fore deck. The third mate came in and told me to keep her head up as we were drifting out of station. A shout from the fo'c'sle head and a pointing finger as a torpedo swept past the bow.

Later, as I lay in my bunk, warm and self satisfied and wearing pyjamas because we were nearly home, there was a roar and a great thump as a ton of cold Atlantic shot down the ventilator straight on to my head. I hung my bedding in the engine room, leaned over the stern rails and watched the convoy rising and falling, stationary to each other but all moving homewards; homewards to a week or two of sleeping peacefully, of not lying looking at the side of the ship wondering what it would be like when it came, of not starting at every thump. Home again to relax in a warm friendly bar, to undress at night, to unwind ready for the next time. 'Home, Home, Home,' the screw threshed the opaque sea. Astern a ship hove to and lowered a boat to pick up a man washed overboard. That night I slept on a bench in

20

the mess room.

We came to Grangemouth on the Forth and were happy for three weeks and forgot. The bos'n went off on leave to the Shetland isles and I understudied for him. Our twelve-pounder gun was removed and in its place we had a beautiful Bofors gun with an army gun crew.

Outward bound again we were delayed at Burnt Island for a few days by the equinoxial gales and when we sailed winter had gone and a weak sun lit our path down the Forth. We came down the northwest coast of Scotland with a red fresh dawn. I stood on the wing of the bridge grasping a scalding mug of tea and was enchanted.

Grey, grey, grey. Back to the Atlantic, to keeping station, to discussing ships, to stress. To St John in Canada for a cargo of grain. But with one warm memory; through the swirling mists of the Newfoundland banks we passed close to a fishing schooner, sails wet and her stern rising gracefully to the following sea. This memory I treasured as I worked twelve hours of overtime at the end of a full day, preparing the shifting boards; for this overtime we got tenpence an hour.

Ashore in the evening we drank harder, more carelessly, not for the fun of drinking but for release. Three days and we were loaded and sailed once more from Halifax. This time we had the commodore of the convoy on board, something we had done before because the *Briarwood* had accommodation for a few passengers. This made little difference to us except that we had to be more formal whilst on the bridge and, because the commodore brought his small staff with him, it put a greater strain on the stewards.

My whole outlook on the war had taken a great change during the hard winter months which we had endured. As I was going to be the target I might as well have the opportunity of doing my share of the shooting. Any vestiges of not fighting a war were now truly gone and I envied my friends who were in the more active branches of the forces. Overriding all this was the fact that being colourblind inhibited me from getting any further at sea than AB or possibly bos'n, and I wanted the opportunity to get further.

During daylight hours one of the crew was always on watch on the monkey island above the bridge and we found that from here we could read, with binoculars, the commodore's convoy plan which he had laid out on the wing of the bridge. Over two or three days, successive lookouts pieced it all together, and we were able to tell the mates quite nonchalantly that so and so was bound for the Clyde, that we were for the Bristol channel, and our old friend over there was going to the Tyne. They refused to believe us until the convoy split up and we were given our orders.

With little over half our journey complete the bulk of our escort took off one night and when day dawned they were no longer with us. Away up in the north the *Hood* had been sunk and even then one or two survivors clung half frozen to floating debris.

A destroyer came alongside with new orders for the commodore. Firing a line across to us they managed to wrap it round the mainstay, where it hung. Reverting to my days in sail I was up the mainmast in a trice and, sliding down the mainstay, I cut the line adrift and brought it back to the deck. While we hauled the container with orders aboard, the destroyer captain made complimentary remarks about our seamanship. A little thing, but it mattered to us in this unglorious North Atlantic bus service.

Nearing home we met up with a U-boat pack one night and they put paid to several ships before our escort drove them off. I lay in my bunk and took my fear pulse and found it quite steady: but why just be the target?

Coming down the Irish Sea in a strong wind the kite snapped the fore topmast and I was dragged swearing from my bunk to go aloft and send it down. Undoubtedly I should have been considerably chagrined had someone else been considered better able to do the job.

We docked in the little harbour of Portishead on the north Somerset coast and were met as usual by His Majesty's Customs who, contrary to recent practice on the northeast, went through the ship with a toothcomb. My share of the £120 fine was some £15 and my father didn't get his usual supply of tobacco.

It was beautiful summer in England now and though things were really tense there was a blessed softness about the country into which we sunk with thankful hearts. Once unloaded we made our way across the Bristol Channel to Cardiff where we lay for some weeks undergoing repairs and getting some leave. One fine morning I was walking in the town enjoying my ease when I came across the Merchant Service Personnel Office, now moved from Tower Hill, and on the spur of the moment entered and asked if I might transfer into the army. The clerk, no doubt underpaid and overworked, sent me about my business with a brief 'No'. Had he wanted to get me into the army he couldn't have acted more wisely.

For three weeks I hunted the bureaucratic machine to find how to change from one service to another, and no one knew the answer. Then one day, reading one of the innumerable pamphlets which war produces, I came across the solution. The port officer was the man. But who was the port officer in this case? Why the harbourmaster, of course. He pulled a little pad from his desk, filled in a form and told me not to try to transfer back.

During my search I had already been assigned to the armoured corps, so now the dye was cast; I had moved from the orbit of one current to another. Now I might know how a normal man set out each day to kill or be killed, how it felt to stand face to face with an enemy knowing that only one of you would survive to tell the tale.

The owners of the *Briarwood* asked me if I would go to navigation school and sit the second mate's exam; they would pay me meanwhile. Being colourblind there was only one answer I could give, but I blessed them for the thought and was sad.

I stood on the quay as the *Briarwood* deep laden with coal, was towed out on her way to New York. She shot down a plane on the way out and on her return was put on the Russian convoys. When the war ended she was still nosing her way across the oceans, her bow still buckled. The men, too, kept with her, demanding so little, enduring stoical and hilarious. I stood a while on the quay in the warm summer sun, lost and friendless, and it was July 1941.

Chapter 2

THREE MONTHS AFTER I joined the army I received a notification that as I had left the Merchant Service I was now liable to be called up for military service.

I travelled down to Tidworth one hot afternoon in mid-August, eager for a new life and rather jaded from the last one, for I had spent the night in London with seafaring acquaintances. This was a part of the country which I knew not at all, as I knew not one thing about the army and its doings. We passed army camps with dust tracks churned by tracked vehicles, khaki trucks and khaki men, huts and signs. Occasionally in the lovely countryside I saw evidence of racing stables and gallops.

We were met at the station by a fleet of trucks and borne away to the taining camp. Immediately we were documented and with some real regret and nostalgia I handed over my seaman's identity card, complete with photograph and fingerprints. We did some intelligence and aptitude tests. One man couldn't read, and so for some months he stoked boilers and led a life of ease on the permanent staff until the sergeant major found him, one chilly autumn morning, sitting happily beside his warm boilers reading the racing in the *Daily Express*. He was posted abroad immediately without training and I have no doubt that he spent the rest of the war happily reading the racing beside some refrigerating plant and collecting campaign medals.

Awkwardly we were marched to our 1901 barrack block, conspicuous in our clothing and sheepishness.

Life began for forty new soldiers, a life which documented us, injected us, fed us, washed us and left no time for reflection. I found that my face was a nuisance; the introductory lecturer explained that it wasn't a case of your face fitting but of being efficient. I smiled in appreciation of the noble sentiments and was sharply reminded to remove the silly grin from off my face. I schooled it into passivity and was pleased with the accomplishment, until one day, standing in line of threes at attention waiting some development, a great roar assailed my ears: 'Take that sneer off your face!' I had no option but to suffer the damn thing and take the consequences. Somehow after I left Tidworth it must have mellowed, for it caused me no more trouble.

My head also was a nuisance for it made no effort to fit the ridiculous side caps which were an essential part of our equipment. Mine fell off with great regularity during foot and arms drill sessions, so that at the end of six weeks' initial training, when inspected before the passing out parade, the troop sergeant had hysterics at its grubby condition and gave me his to wear. While marching and counter-marching it left me and was tramped firmly into the parade ground. This difficulty was solved when I bought myself a black beret.

We were a motley crowd from all walks of life, though most of us had some skill or profession which had delayed our call up and in consequence at 24 years old I was one of the youngest. Dick was over 40 and had been a man of considerable consequence in the customs service in China and received deference from officers and men alike, much to his fury. There were schoolmasters and pharmacists, shoe operatives and stockbrokers' clerks, three wealthy young men destined for officer training, mechanics and poachers. Almost without exception they were eager and ready to train and then to fight, not with any romantic fervour but because the job had to be finished before they could return to normal life, or so they thought. In fact not one could return to normal life, for those who returned were not the same men. While they fought, struggled and died they had a dream of life as it should be and saw a side of the human soul which was finer than anything they had known. When they returned to a drab and spiritless Britain they didn't abandon themselves to disillusion but locked away their dream so that none should laugh it to scorn. Sometimes behind those eyes it comes to light.

The late summer and autumn were gorgeous and though life was really energetic and demanding we enjoyed it. We were impressed with the training we received. We became very fit through constant drill and PT and were always hungry, every meal a pleasure in consequence. On Saturday afternoons we went into Salisbury with the few shillings we received to try to regain our individuality for a few hours. I spent four afternoons in a bookshop reading a book which I couldn't afford to buy. The pubs were so crowded that you could only get a drink if you had a glass; one pub even boasted sandwiches—which were plain bread with a piece of pickled beetroot inside. Around the camp there were canteens and dances, which passed the time for some.

There was also a library, but I found little energy for reading. Doped with air and exercise we became happily animal in outlook. I tried to think about what we were doing and why, and how I should prepare myself to meet whatever came. I lay one Sunday afternoon on my bunk and tried to reason out why we had to take a perfectly good pair of boots and polish them until they were brittle and useless. The reason was obvious, but I was still committed to the notion of total war. In only one respect have I any criticism of the training we received. We were not being prepared to face injury and therefore the shock effects were much greater when they came. Some people prepared themselves, some had a gradual introduction, but those who were thrown suddenly into the maelstrom often suffered.

After six weeks we had finished our initial training and set off for ten days' leave like new boys at the end of their first term; all except a stockbroker's clerk who could not perform drill with his rifle sufficiently skilfully. Bashfully we arrived at out separate homes in uniform, which though quite normal at Tidworth seemed so crude and gross in the home. On return we were sent to our specialist training: driver, gunner or radio operator. We spent weeks with a pair of headphones over our ears taking down and sending messages in Morse, a code which I used only once after my training was over. Besides this we learnt to operate a wireless set, to maintain it simply and the procedures for using it. There were only a small group of us and we were drilled remorselessly until we really knew our job. Most of the work was done in bare little rooms in old houses which had been married quarters in the days of peace. At half past ten each day we broke off from our tasks and repaired to the nearest NAAFI for a mug of tea and wad. As the radio burst forth into 'Music While You Work' we returned to our duties. I dreamed of the day when I was so free that I could hear the music; such are our simple dreams.

Occasionally we went out in the wireless trucks doing schemes round the lovely Wiltshire countryside, with sandwiches in a pub for lunch. Interspersed with our programme we did our stint of PT, fatigues and drill parades. As we marched in column of threes towards our barrack block, the sergeant-major would be roaring 'On parade' before we had even arrived to change our clothing for the next task. I don't think anyone was very worried over this sort of thing. As civilians we took from the army what we thought was necessary and ignored the bull.

One day we were all told off to do an intelligence paper. It was explained by the educational sergeant that it was felt that intelligent men were doing trivial tasks and unintelligent men had tasks of some importance. This hardly seemed a startling discovery. However, everyone from the OC to the newest recruit did these tests. We heard no more until one night the guard, becoming accustomed to the army and being bored, searched the orderly room and found the results tabulated. Not surprisingly they had been shoved to the back of a drawer. I applied for a commission and was summoned in front of the OC, who told me to get some experience with a regiment and then apply again. I was surprised at being turned down, because I would have been a good officer. However, it meant a much quicker posting and I appreciated that experience of real war would be an advantage.

We all passed out from the wireless wing and started a gunnery course on the Besa machine gun and the two-pounder tank gun. Again this was very well taught and we knew our subject. It was at this point that we actually sat in a tank crawling around the plain, aiming and traversing the gun. Christmas came and a tremendous effort was made to see that we all got our Christmas dinner. It was a nice gesture but home without the dinner would have been very different from dinner without home. In fact we didn't get our dinner on Christmas Day because the cookhouse ran out of food and we had to feed on Boxing Day instead.

We went down to Castle Martin in Pembrokeshire to do our firing practice, leaving Tidworth dusted with snow and bitterly cold to reach the balmy coasts of the Atlantic. It was nice to see the sea again. Another hurdle finished and we only had a brief course in driving and maintenance. I enjoyed sitting in the back of an army truck smoking my pipe and looking at the frozen countryside glittering in the sun. By the end of February it was all over. I was a trained soldier officially going on leave for fourteen days prior to embarkation—for where?

I enjoyed my leave at home, simply and quietly. There was a heightened enjoyment of all the simple things with no pretences at a gay life. Living in a small boarding school full of life, vitality and joy there were no quiet fits of brooding, nor the energy for despair. I found leaving easier than that time when I had gone back to the ship with a Canadian address in my pocket, until I came out through the front door on to the front step and met a host of small boys there to wish me well. I carried it off, but only just.

A draft was gathered together at Tidworth, made up of people from all sorts of regiments in the armoured corps and some of us who had just finished our training. I sat and heard 'Music While You Work' and then became bored with just sitting. We drew our tropical kit, including an Imperial pith helmet in a khaki bag and long shorts with huge turn-ups which would cover the knee when let down. They were commonly known as 'dysentry shorts'. Apart from this we appeared to have a reasonable and sensible kit. We attended lectures, were examined medically and generally paraded to the satisfaction of all.

It was dark when we fell in, dressed in greatcoats, hung with packs, valises and water bottles and carrying a kit bag with a small khaki bag attached containing our imperial headgear. We didn't march, but we advanced through the dark towards the railway sidings. A NAAFI girl out with another eager escort shouted her blessings. So trite and mundane, yet we felt that in her simple heart she really meant it, and we were happy that someone cared.

Chapter 3

WE SUFFERED THE unending journey to the Clyde, jammed in a carriage with all our equipment and nowhere to put it. As we didn't know where we were going, nor when we should arrive, we dozed in a state of limbo, an essential ability necessary for survival when part of a huge organisation. Festooned with equipment, and with an occasional Imperial dig in the back, we were ferried out to our troopship, the *Empire Pride*. Up and up the companion ladder to the deck, down down the companion ladder to a troop deck in the bowels of the ship: a large deck at the very bottom of the fore hold; rows of tables and benches bolted to the deck; overhead slatted racks for our equipment; at right-angles pipework for securing our hammocks; occasionally a slatted locker for stowing hammocks and bedding. Electric light, force draught ventilation, no portholes. Simple, adequate, minimal. With some experience behind me I chose a hammock space immediately beneath a force draught vent and said nothing to anyone about it. War after all is finally a case of personal survival.

Quickly and efficiently we were divided up, instructed in procedure and apportioned to different tasks. We drew our supper from the galley and sat at our table enjoying the novelty. There was an air of exhilaration and expectancy. Our deck was now full of its assorted complement of soldiers, drawn from all corps, of varying experience and from every walk of life. We slung our hammocks, so that the whole deckhead sagged with recumbent figures; below them on the deck stretched figures luxuriating on mattresses. Apart from a pair of feet rubbing each ear, and two separate ears squeezing your feet, the hammock was comfortable. I blessed the force draught ventilation. In the blue gloom of the night time lighting, figures crept bent double beneath the hammocks, stepping surreptitiously past sleeping bodies on the deck on their way to the heads. A weak bladder is not a help on a troopship.

At an early hour we were on the move. In the wash rooms the crowd was packed solid for several hours; below a desperate writhing struggle to roll up hammocks, dress in your own clothes and disentangle your equipment. And then the moment of release when we staggered on to the deck and could gulp down some real fresh air and stand free and untouched by another human body. The army in its wisdom did not over organise, but left the problems to the humans who had to face them, so that over the next eight weeks we evolved a life that saw us disembark in sanity. True we all disembarked wearing each other's clothing and equipment, but we were still sane and able to stand. Some men didn't bother to sleep at night but played cards, scrounged cups of tea or queued in the wash room for a bottle of water with which to wash. Some slept early and rose early, some slept late and rose late. Such is the genius of the unorganised British.

Once we had breakfasted we were driven up on deck where we stood like a herd of bullocks in a desolate field. We had a parade, because this is always something you can do when all else fails. Right across the foredeck below the bridgehouse was a large and luxuriant-looking saloon, the windows of which looked straight into our pasture. We gazed with cow-like eyes and steamy breath at officers reclining in deep chairs, and waiters bearing trays of drinks. We didn't resent the officers their comfort but we didn't want it shoved down our throats. Nor were we as impressed when it was announced over the public address system that, because of the urgency of the situation, we were carrying 30 per cent extra men. That evening I was put on a detail which was to keep submarine watch from various vantage points of the ship; this was a true stroke of fortune, for it meant watch keeping, freeing us from any routine fatigues and giving us the run of the ship. Given 2,500 men crowded on board and totally ignorant of ships it was only necessary to mutter something half technical and the way was cleared.

We sailed out into the Atlantic in convoy with a formidable escort. Before we had cleared the influence of the land I was sleeping peacefully with my head pillowed in two pairs of feet. I awoke to the gentle pitch and roll of a long Atlantic swell, the sound of water surging passed the steel plates of our dungeon, the gentle hum of machinery buried even deeper, and a sight that only Hogarth could have captured.

No gin palace ever held such an orgy of misery as I saw before me. Figures in hammocks, out of hammocks, half in and half out; bodies lying abandoned on the deck, bodies sitting at the tables with heads proffered to the block. And the stench! Fortunately I was on watch and went quietly and swiftly to my station at the stern where the air was clean and I could watch the wake of the ship rolling away behind me as we headed out into the Atlantic. When I returned a miracle had been wrought and all was normal, apart from a few figures recumbent at the tables. Later in the morning, in search of someone for the troop sergeant, I entered the heads, which filled a vast area under an extended fo'c'sle head. Down the middle ran two long troughs, built as urinals but now flanked on either side by a row of khaki behinds. I searched in vain and suggested mildly to the sergeant, on reporting my failure, that all troops on board should have their name, rank and number stencilled on the seat of their trousers.

The British soldier is a resilient animal so that within two days he no longer had to joke about his agony; it was forgotten and he was busy making himself at home in these strange conditions. I found this extremely trying, because firstly I heard on all sides such a wealth of inaccurate information passed from the know-alls to those around them that I could have screamed, and secondly housey-housey, or bingo as it is now called, reared its awful head. It spread throughout the ship as more and more syndicates received permits to run games, they continued all day and all night. Only when I was on watch did I escape. At night in alleyways catering staff sold tea and sandwiches at fancy prices and furtive characters conducted games of crown and anchor. By day we could at least breathe fresh air and look at the sea or the ships around us, but once darkness fell we were herded below. At least we could forget in crowded sleep.

The food, which we had enjoyed at first, began to pall. Perhaps we were jaded without exercise, perhaps the cooks working against all odds were jaded. As is the normal army custom an orderly officer arrived at each meal supported by an orderly sergeant, whose task it was to bring the assembled company to order and bellow 'Any complaints'. On one particular day the sergeant arrived with a newly commissioned young officer and posed his usual query. At the far end of the deck a figure arose from his bench bearing some small object hanging from a fork. The noise stilled, heads peered and followed his course towards the officer. He arrived with a small rabbit's kidney, which he had rescued from his soup, dangling from a piece of skin transfixed by his fork. Drawing himself up respectfully he held this forward and gravely said: 'Sir, I think someone had dropped a bollock.' The howl of pagan joy that greeted his sally blew across the convoy, echoing down into the southern oceans.

One day, needing my lunch early because of my watch keeping, I arrived in the galley and was served by the labouring cooks. 'Any sweet?' 'Yes, please.' He opened the steam oven and drew out a steam pudding in a bowl. Releasing the captive pudding from the bowl he picked up a large cleaver and struck it a cruel blow, presumably to cut it. With surprising elasticity it parried his thrust but was thrown to the deck in the struggle, where it bounced once and was still. 'No sweet, thank you.'

As we steamed south the weather grew balmy and we changed into 'dysentry shorts' and shirts. Surreptitiously the scissors got to work and we rid ourselves of 'dysentry' and appeared in shorts.

The convoy put into Freetown for a few days, but this affected our life in no way. I was on submarine look out when we anchored inside the torpedo net in the harbour, so seeing the officer i/c submarines I asked if we should suspend look out while in port. 'No, indeed we must continue.' That night, as I stood on the wing of the boat deck searching the harbour for submarines against the bright lights of the ship and the harbour, I was hauled over the coals by a major. 'You're very scruffy,' he said. 'Yes, Sir,' I replied. So he went away. On again: housey housey, crown and anchor, bouncing sweet.

Eventually we put into Durban and the Tidworth draft were put ashore. We had apparently been bound for Singapore but that had fallen before we rounded the Cape. We moved out to heaven, the camp at Clarewood, where we slept in tents, showered to excess, ate like human beings and were so kindly treated by the people that this became the land of the lotus-eaters. The first night six of us were taken down to a warehouse in the docks to mount a guard. On inspection it contained the kit of men killed in the Middle East which was awaiting shipment home; not an exciting duty.

Most of our time was free and as I had an uncle living on the outskirts and a flat full of charming cousins living in the town, life was idyllic. I compounded to take a cousin to the races at Clarewood on the Easter Monday, but the army intervened. They obviously considered, perhaps with some justification, that we were eating too many lotuses. On Easter Saturday we paraded with small packs and groundsheets and marched off to 'The Valley of a Thousand Hills', which is I believe quite a tourist attraction. Over the weekend we marched up each hill and slept at night in the pouring rain. Monday afternoon came and there was panic. Our ship had arrived. It was hurry, hurry, hurry; we were foot sore and bolshie and there wasn't any hurry. In fact we did not embark until Tuesday midday.

The ship was a very large French liner in which our conditions were good. We entered the dining saloon, still resplendent with some of its peacetime décor, and sat down to eat. Down a passageway between the tables fled a member of the crew, followed swiftly by an adversary brandishing a large cleaver which he hurled with all his might.

We lived in a space that had been a loading point for supplies. It had a steel door opening in the side of the ship and being well above sea level we could have this open, which gave us light and a strong fresh breeze. As I lay in my hammock smoking gently and reminiscing about the joys of lotus land, a voice at my side said 'Can you ride a motor bike?' 'Yes,' I said dreamily. 'You're on mess-room fatigues,' the voice said. And so I was.

As all the men ate in the dining saloon there was one

36

unending meal—breakfast, lunch, supper—as one finished the next began. I had a table to look after and life was an unending round of collect the food, wash up, collect the food. Half way up the Red Sea I collected a large boil and went back to my hammock.

The only blot on board was that although the ship was dry to other ranks, sergeants and upwards could drink. I wasn't worried by the lack of drink, but I gladly joined in when we wheeled a piano into the officers' mess and sang the 'Red Flag'. Beer was on sale the next day.

Another journey over we were loaded into dusty railway coaches travelling across to Cairo. It was late when we reached the barracks, so we bedded down on the floor in the cool airy barrack room. We had arrived another step nearer the war.

Chapter 4

I AWOKE VERY early despoiled and besmirched; I felt one mass of bites. As I ran my hand over my face and neck I found range after range of mountains where the night before there was nothing but smooth skin. I lay fretting and disgusted until it grew light, when I got up and showered in cool clean water. Restored and forewarned I was ready to meet whatever might come.

We found ourselves in a large permanent camp with every sort of facility for a pleasant life within the limits of army routine. Canteens of every sort abounded and our constant thirst was catered for on every side and in simple surroundings. Under a tree a group of small rickety tables and some chairs; cold fresh lemon and water drunk from a thick green glass which had started life as a beer bottle; small cool buildings with an encircling veranda; dim thick-walled old stone buildings where you could sit quite still and forget the heat. There were *dhobi* men who returned your khaki shirts and shorts, stiff and immaculate with starch, six hours after they had been handed in. At the main gate a stall, open most of the night, selling fried egg or chicken sandwiches. Outside was Cairo, a major city overrun with troops of all sorts and from many nations: from Britain and Australia, New Zealand and South Africa, Rhodesia, the sub-continent of India, Poland, Greece and France. Behind every soldier ran a small Arab boy trying to sell him something; in front ran another little boy trying to clean his boots. Through the thousands of cafés and restaurants roamed Arabs selling razor blades, sunglasses, postcards, pens and bric-à-brac. A disproportionate number of shops sold watches, and a disproportionate number of watches were stolen. Thousands of careless men roamed the city in short-sleeved shirts; it was all too easy to snatch the watch from an arm hanging carelessly from a passing tram; to walk beside an arm quietly cutting the strap with a razor blade. It was vivid, loud and garish, which was just what the troops wanted when returning from the desert. We enjoyed it on the money which we had acquired while travelling out.

Once established it was back to training again. At 5.30 in the morning we had swallowed a cup of tea and were tethered round a cool whitewashed classroom taking down Morse in a stupefied way. When we left at 7.30 there were always some characters sitting erect, headphones in place, dreaming of a gentler start to the day. After a breakfast more lessons; as most of the tanks currently in use in the desert were American we had to learn the mechanism of totally new guns. Lunch was occasionally followed by drill or PT but usually we lay in the shade until the cool of the afternoon, when we gently prepared ourselves for a night of frolic.

Behind all this gay and casual life was an earnestness and eagerness to get up the desert. We were told to try to cut down on our drinking to become used to the meagre ration we should receive later, and suffered agonies while surrounded by so many pleasant drinking spots. We dredged what information we could from our fellows who had served with units in the desert; we talked and thought. Since we joined the army we had been quite carefree, doing what we were told, going and coming, meek and resilient, bearing no responsibility, tied hand and foot and yet in many ways utterly free.

Now this was ending, for to the west there were angry men and dead men and wounded men. There we should know what we were, how we would conduct ourselves. There we should not be free for we must control our minds and bodies in conditions impossible to visualise. This was what had quietly driven me to the army; I saw this now. How did a normal easy-going man feel when quite literally face to face with an enemy knowing that one or the other must die? It seems unreasonable that man should be able to do it; obviously quite ordinary men did. Should I learn. . . .?

We were just settling down to a gentle life of luxury when the call came. We handed in all unnecessary equipment including the Imperial hat which had not yet been worn, drew a revolver and paraded fully accoutred. Beret, shirt, shorts, stockings and short puttees and boots; besides this a khaki pullover and a greatcoat, packs large and small, water bottle, revolver and bed roll. We were loaded into a simple train and set off, rattling westwards on our wooden seats. Through the irrigated area, past ditches etched with rushes, buffalo working the simple irrigation pumps, little villages of squalid flat-roofed houses, and fields and fields and fields. Slowly we went and slowly out of the irrigated area to the sand and scrub and dust. The occasional camp with a permanent hut or two and rows of well-worn tents; dusty tracks turning into dust clouds at the approach of a vehicle. With us we took a swarm of flies, which pried and bit around our eyes, nostrils and mouth, forever crawling and buzzing, never relenting, true descendants of Moses' plague.

At some point the train halted and we climbed out, down the embankment and across to a cookhouse sitting in a sandy waste where a South African coloured unit fed trainloads of dusty soldiers. We bore off a mess tin of mealie porridge and corn beef and half a mug of tea;

40

wonderful tea, slightly dusted with fine sand, but still the only real thirst quencher. We squatted down and ate, washed our utensils arbitrarily in an old four-gallon petrol can of hot water, and were on our way. Some time in the evening we disembarked and were loaded into goods waggons, crowded with our kit into an uncomfortable heap, Through the night we stretched and kicked ourselves a cramped space. Poor Bill, who had gippo tummy, spent the night hanging crouched out of the sliding doors attending to the violence of his bowels and using his precious piastre notes in place of toilet paper. Hurrah for the hundreds of thousands of local papers, sent to keep the boys in touch with home affairs, for the army didn't provide paper and it didn't grow in the desert.

The rail head came with a grey bleak dawn: a flat stretch of gravelly sand, a few sad tents dotted far apart for fear of bombing and an immense stretch of scruffy nothingness. We disembarked and stood stretching and cold beside the waggons. Blowing across the waste were clouds of fine sand. Some South Africans appeared through the yellow haze, greatcoated and dusty, and lay down behind a mound of baggage. The line just ended and there was nothing.

As the day wore on we fed on cool greasy bacon powdered with fine grit, hard biscuits and cool tea; the top of the tea was greasy with a scum of fine sand. Trucks arrived, the sun came through the haze and we were borne away from this desolation into the heat of the day, along the coast road, past Sollum lying tranquil beside an unutterably beautiful sea, and up the pass into Cyrenaica. On our left a high bare escarpment, the road running at its foot; to our right flat scrubby land running away to a bluff coastline. We passed the charming little port of Bahdia and soon after turned right into a reinforcement camp.

There was no cover in the desert so the only protection against air attack was to disperse over as wide an area as possible. Also there was no lack of room and in consequence tents were spread far apart, each solitary from its fellows. We were dropped outside the office tent and stood, dusty and dishevelled, wilting slowly in the extreme heat. Our induction was brief and cursory: we found a tent and we had a new home for the moment. There was no room for pomposity with this brilliant hard heat beating on a land, severe and complete. Man was unnecessary here and seemed to feel it.

We had nothing to do now but to wait and to acclimatise physically and mentally. Each morning we paraded rather arbitrarily, a few duties were allocated, we did a sweep of the desert in extended formation, picking up rubbish exposed by yesterday's wind, and returned to our tents where there was shade. Lying in shorts only, sweating gently and rough with fine sand, we talked and waited the next drink. At breakfast, lunch and supper we walked a quarter of a mile to the cookhouse tent, received our due in a mess tin and half a mug of tea and walked back the quarter mile to the shade of the tent. Initially we had drunk the tea before we reached the shade. Breakfast was fat, greasy bacon with a few beans or a more substantial sausage called a soya link, a vast solid sausage devoid of any meat or flavour, but a meal to the hungry, and we were. Occasionally we had some bread, more often hard biscuits, which I preferred because the bread was always rather dry and it was easier to blow the sand off the biscuits. Lunch was biscuits and cheese, some yellow liquid that had been margarine and—horror of horrors—a sweet glutinous mess called fig jam, which came from Palestine. Supper was corn beef stew: corn beef boiled in water with some tinned potatoes. It must have been a pretty successful diet, for we were always hungry enough to eat whatever was put before us and enjoy it. We grew lean and hard.

One night the camp was straffed by a passing Jerry plane, without damage, but we were all ordered to dig the tents in two to three feet so that we were lying below ground level. There was a singeing hot wind blowing across the land as we toiled and sweated to break through rock-hard areas and to shovel away the accumulated load of sand. By afternoon we were so desperate for drink that we dropped all pretence at work and set off down the steep escarpment to a little wadi which ran down to the sea, where there was a spring of sorts. We filled an old jerrycan, drank our fill too fast and staggered back bearing our forbidden prize. All the afternoon we worked and drank; by evening we lay safely in our tent, our bellies replete and splashing with water, our thirst still rampant. This was a turning point and though on other occasions we were very thirsty we contained our desires and learnt to do without.

This had been an Italian area before the Wavell push up the desert and the wadis round were filled with litter and workings from their occupation; they had spent considerable trouble making their sojourn as pleasant as possible. One midday I went alone to poke about. The land burned with a fierce heat and great solid waves hit me, but I didn't wither. I realised with joy and fierce pride that I could stand upright, unbowed and resilient; I could enjoy the endlessness, the simplicity and the hardness of this proud and distant land.

Our time passed. In the tent we had a cockney who regaled us with tales of petty theft and sharp practice, which to him were the very essence of life. Daily we went down to the sea and swam; scruffy waifs enjoying this millionaires' beach. One day to our excitement a submarine surfaced in the bay and made off along the coast.

But the war restarted beyond Tobruk and the coast

road was thick with traffic. Tanks moved past ceaselessly up the road; supplies poured past and excitement mounted. This time we should win; Jerry was trapped; confidence was unbridled. We chafed to be in it before it was all over. Daily small drafts went out to make up depleted regiments. One dreadful morning I was detailed as batman; this meant being on the camp staff. I knew that I just happened to be detailed by accident because of my position in the row, so I drew myself up and said: 'No, I joined the army to fight.' To my amazement the sergeant-major merely detailed the man next to me. Finally the moment came. Six of us reduced our kit still further, donned our gear and climbed in a truck bound up to Tobruk. Now I should know what it felt like.

The land shimmered in the heat, lakes shone brilliantly where we knew there was nothing but sand and gravel, stunted bushes grew and wavered as the heat distorted the light waves. I rejoiced in it; was I not now a member seared to an erect immunity? We were deposited at a scruffy little camp beside the El Adem airfield; just a small tent, some sand and a few bodies waiting to be sent where they would. The heat of the battle was on; caution now joined optimism. The army commander arrived in his car and made encouraging noises. After an eternity off we went in a truck to a supply depot and took over a Stewart tank. A driver, an enormous ex-gunner, myself and a corporal who had come out on the draft from Tidworth, we checked what we could, stowed our gear and laid out our beds on the sand at the side of the tank. We were going up to the Gloucestershire Yeomanry in the morning.

Before the sun was up we were off with an officer to show us the way. The air was cold and fresh and we shivered as we threaded our way through the maze of tracks, always chased by our thick cloud of dust. We stripped the covers off the guns; tense, stomachs empty but without hunger. This I had yearned for; was I equal to it? We arrived at nowhere: a patch of sand, a map reference. I was told to net my wireless set to the regiment; in vain I went through the procedure, but with no response. Confused with embarrassment I reported my failure; was I so hopeless? A corporal came over, tried without result, and to my relief he reported the set out of order. Signals would come to mend it. We sat there all day, alone, discarded. The corporal asked me to make the set unworkable so that we could return to safer pastures. Livid with contempt I lost my fear and waited calmly. Later, much later, I met the corporal in command of a water truck—a round peg in a round hole. Even then some fighting man was debarred from promotion because this oaf held the position of corporal in the regiment.

We sat on a flat stretch, to one side the lip of a depression sloping down to the battle area, to where the Germans should have been contained but weren't, for they were busy breaking out at the south end. Tanks came to the lip and disappeared from sight, but not from sound, for we could hear the firing and at times see the tracer from a shot that came too far. On our other side sappers were steadily laying a minefield in spite of constant attacks by dive bombers. We sat and waited, unknowing and unwanted. At midday on the next day we were told to take the tank back to Tobruk, because the regiment was coming out of the line. Unknown to us they had suffered very severe casualties and were in fact joined to a sister regiment soon after.

A mass of vehicles were on their way back and the journey was tedious. We reported at an ordnance depot and handed over the tank. Where the corporal and driver went I do not know, but the gunner and I asked directions from an ordnace major, who having listened to our story pointed out that we had been written off the books of the reinforcement camp and had obviously not been put on the strength of the Gloucesters. He suggested that we go back to the delta and get a boat home. We walked round to Tobruk, which was preparing in a casual way for another siege, wondering whether to join some unit there of our own accord or whether to make our way back to a reinforcement camp. Late afternoon found us riding on a tank transporter eastwards.

With a great mass of men from all sorts of armoured units we found a camp, reported in, chose a bed space in a tent and waited. All the next day we waited lying in a tent trying to contain our thirst; with the huge influx of bodies water was very short. We found a jerrycan full of water red with rust which must have fallen from some vehicle in a previous campaign. We drank it with pleasure.

There followed what seemed weeks of moving camp ever eastwards as the army fell back towards the delta. We knew nothing and only wished to stand and fight, if we knew where or with what. Two days here, one day there, but always moving; we earned our keep pitching and striking camp. I managed to worm my way on to a training tank and travelled with that. The coast road was a never-ending stream of vehicles retreating; it could take hours to cross on foot. One evening as we drove along the rough ground at the side of the road the tank driver, trying to keep one track on the road and one on a bank, reached the point where the tank was about to tip on its side on to the road. Those of us riding leapt off as he stopped and we spent many many weary hours of that night digging the bank away. To have blocked the road at that point in time would have been disastrous.

As we passed El Alamein we saw troops digging in; there was order and troops moving up from the delta.

Encouraged, though shamefaced at taking a tank the wrong way, we pressed on. Finally we met up with our unit again, camped happily beside the road and separated from the sea shore by a row of palm trees. There was water and we could wash the thick layer of dust from our bodies, eat quietly and lie on our blankets beside the tank, clean, weary and content. We had acquired some whisky, which we drank slowly and reverently from the bottle, lying back in the cool watching a great, brilliant moon climb slowly higher. As the bottle got lighter I found to my immense joy that I could see two bright round moons. I lay and enjoyed this added luxury, now and then eliminating one moon merely by closing one eye. I was very happy but had signally failed in my search.

The following weeks were misery as I got enmeshed further and further in the reinforcement camp, which moved sporadically and apparently without reason. I, who desperately wished to get into the line, was left languishing, while hundreds of reluctant men were sent forward. Doing nothing for long periods is desperately wearying, and the army's insistence on always giving you the exact opposite of what you desired I found so exasperating that I was in the mood for a private mutiny. Finally I asked for an interview with the OC and we discovered that I was not on the list from which they made their postings.

With new heart I started to wait again. The camp appeared bearable; with a heart now devoid of fury I looked about me with renewed interest. At one side of us in the steep slope was cut an archway through the rock, leading to a little amphitheatre open to the sky above. Around this amphitheatre were small caves, where lived some Arabs, and here came little caravans of camels and donkeys bearing their loads. To me the whole was putrid with the filth of centuries, but to these people this was a refuge while they went about their centuries-old life unhurried by the lunacies of the white man. One day, while emptying the stones from an old four-gallon petrol tin, a snake fell on my wrist and to the ground. An Arab nearby, shouting diabolically, ran up and smote it with a large stave. I thanked him profusely, while he performed a pantomime on the evils of this creature.

At last I was posted to 1st Tank Regiment.

Chapter 5

FOUR OF US sat in the back of a fifteen hundred-weight truck as we made our way along the winding tracks; in places where the sand was too soft steel mesh had been laid. Ominously the flies kept up with us, forever probing for the soft spots in the corners of the eyes, the mouth and the nostrils. Behind us billowed a cloud of dust, which gently rained a fine powder over our heads and faces. A pillar of cloud by day and a plague of flies: how little the world had altered. Along the track we passed sign boards bearing queer cryptic messages in initial letters, designating the unit in occupation of that piece of wasteland: some trucks widely dispersed, the odd camouflage net draped, a few bivvies dug into the sand, very occasionally a man. Further and further south we bounced and jolted, arriving with the evening cool at the forward supply echelon to be deposited on the bare empty desert, alone, homeless, friendless, abandoned.

This was a pattern repeated over and over; men arriving alone and solitary, outcasts, the descendants of Cain. Yet within very few days they had attached themselves, their loyalty, their very affection to a truck, tank or gun, because this was the core of a little group of outcasts, supporting and encompassing one another. The desert army was broken up into thousands and thousands of little groups whose very core was a fire tin and a brew can. As the factories churned out their stream of cheap disposable petrol cans they little realised that their poor utilitarian manufactures became our penates, the bond round which we lived, our means of a communal being, our means of offering hospitality. The fire tin—tall, rectangular with lid removed and holes punched in the side, into which sand was poured and on to the sand petrol—primitive, messy and highly effective. The brew tin was merely a smaller section of the same type of tin with a piece of wire for a handle. These two blackened objects hung and swayed behind every desert vehicle of the allied armies, a silent endorsement of the statement that 'Our lads had the finest equipment in the world'. Often even less of a petrol tin acted the part of frying pan.

Quickly we were assimilated into this new nomadic group. Firstly we attached ourselves to a truck which gave us our penates, our transport, address and our *raison d'être*. Then we became known, passing gossip of our military career to date during the long hours which stretched empty through the heat of the day. Very soon we felt we belonged, so that in the evening, when queuing outside the cookhouse truck which came up from the rear echelon bearing wet bully beef stew and tinned potatoes, we could pass the time of day with members of the other vehicles and tanks that collected together for mutual protection in the night.

Just before sunrise we rose, rolled our bedding, loaded up and drove away to our solitary stations, to spend the day waiting on events, free from the dangers of air attack on a concentrated group. We stood around the stationary vehicles, subdued and rather chill, watching the sky in the east go red and the orb of the sun rise up from the horizon. As it came clear the fire tin was at the ready and the moment the light was strong enough fires billowed all around the desert and a new day began.

Two days passed in peace and then Rommel made his final bid for the delta. The tanks sat in their appointed places and waited; we sat on our secluded plateau and waited. Now there was tension in the air, yet calm and confidence. The day wore on, with much increased air activity and the distant sound of artillery and small arms fire. Late in the afternoon we could hear our own tanks firing and as the intensity of the light declined there was a veritable firework display from the armour-piercing shot floating back and forth. This was not something detached; each streak of light was a shot capable of the destruction of a tank, the mutilation of the crew or the incineration of the whole. I drew in my breath sharply and audibly, so that a sergeant standing beside me dropped his hand on my shoulder and said simply: 'You get used to it.'

That night when it was dark I went up with the supply trucks and took my place as wireless operator on the regimental navigator's tank. My predecessor greeted me, gave me some very brief instructions and left. I unrolled my bed and lay down beside my new colleagues, strange, separate and nervous. The air was cool and the stars were bright in the heavens above, tranquil in their ageless immensity. I slept. A shaken shoulder, a few quiet words and it was turn for guard duty. A quick struggle into pullover and boots, a check on the tommy gun, and the night was yours: barely was one guard on his feet than the other was asleep. Time was gentle on these serene nights and soon it was my turn to shake a shoulder and slide back into the ecstasy of warm blankets and oblivion. The crackle of small-arms fire from the infantry out in front only made my bed the more secure.

In the chill of pre-dawn we were up, dressed, beds rolled and lashed to the tank, engine running while I crouched over the wireless to re-tune and answer my call sign. Daylight found us all in position; the sun arose and quickly warmed us. On the wireless I listened as A squadron, in light tanks, probed quietly outwards to find Jerry; he had withdrawn leaving a litter of blackened and broken hulks. Tension relaxed and we and the heavy squadrons gave our thoughts to breakfast. Fire tins blazed and as the first mug of hot, thick tea was sipped gingerly, beans and bacon were fried.

Time moved slowly for us in our little wadi: the colonel's tank, 2nd in command, adjutant, navigator and the intelligence officer in his scout car. We could see nothing except the steep sandy sides and above a cloudless sky with a brilliant sun. The wireless hummed endlessly as the light tanks moved quietly and gently forward, probing. I listened as they got in and out of trouble, the flies buzzed and probed remorselessly and at regular intervals a flight of 18 Boston medium bombers flew over in immaculate formation. There was a low thunder, the quick crack of heavy AA fire, and rising into the sky a pall of smoke.

The day passed slowly and quietly; occasionally a shell whistled by, way above us in our snug. I got to know my colleagues. Quiet, competent and experienced, Harry the sergeant was a regular and had been fighting up and down the desert for nearly two years, while Dingo the driver and Eddy the gunner were part of the civilian army and had spent a year of to and fro. The day wore slowly on to a sinking sun and the cool of evening. Darkness came fast and with it the supply wagons, ammunition, water rations and hot bully stew and rather stiff and withdrawn characters such as myself of the night before. Today I was part of it, my troubles were at an end.

Tension relaxed, but still we remained on instant readiness, while the Germans withdrew and the air force kept up its pounding. One day the Luftwaffe visited with a swarm of dive bombers. Eddy and I and Dingo were on the turret with the AA gun thoroughly enjoying ourselves until the planes suddenly dived down towards us and from their undersides fell the dark sinister canisters. Dingo and I took a jump and a dive and were safely underneath the tank before the detonations in a neighbouring wadi. We crawled out rather shamefaced to meet Eddy grinning broadly. By the following day the attack was finished, and throughout the desert armies there was a feeling of jubilation and, more important, a great rise in confidence. For a few days more we remained in our positions and I became an established part.

Life for us really evolved round the disposable four-gallon petrol tin, for this was the motive power behind the whole army; on it depended our very lives, for without the water waggons we should soon have perished. From the depots in the delta a never-ending chain of lorries ploughed and bumped their way up the desert to rear petrol dumps, to forward petrol dumps, to rear supply echelons, to forward supply echelons, to the troops at the front. Being flimsy containers the wastage was terrifying and it was quite common to see petrol oozing out of the back of a truck. The Germans, on the other hand, had a well designed, well constructed, robust container which did continuous service and which later on was introduced to the allied armies under the name of 'jerrican'. What should we have done had our war effort been as carefully planned? Where would be our fire tin, our brew tin, our frying pan, wash tin, our loo, a marker on desert tracks, a post box. It was the great provider; the one article in plentiful supply. From it we derived our mobility and also our furnishings.

Water was our other preoccupation and although I was rarely desperate for water there were many times when I was thinking of nothing else. We very seldom drank water as such for it was lukewarm, chlorinated and sometimes quite salty, and did little to quench our thirst or remove the fine layer of dust from our throats. Tea was the great elixir; strong thick tea greasy with evaporated milk and powdered with dust. If really hot it brought you out in a glorious sweat that cooled as it evaporated in the dry heat. Water was used for washing but very very sparingly or after the lucky find of a lost or abandoned can. I washed every day with a pint mug part full. First I washed my teeth, spitting the water back into the mug. Then I shaved, washed my face, and dipping a slimy flannel into the sludge washed myself down. Clothes we normally washed in our old friend and comforter petrol, which reduced the drudgery, dried almost instantly and also killed any vermin which might be travelling with you.

Personal possessions were minimal: a spare shirt, shorts and perhaps socks, means of washing, shaving and drying, a pencil, eating irons, mess tin and mug and a roll of dusty blankets in which lived an overcoat and pullover for the chill nights. I have never accustomed myself since to the plethora of possessions deemed necessary for modern life. To be able to pick up your whole accumulation of wordly goods and walk off gives a great sense of freedom, something which the dropouts from society have always known and something we all learned and then forgot.

Our life was quite elemental, ordered, simple and mentally numbing. We rose shortly before the sun, rolled our bedding and strapped it on the back of the tank, warmed the engine and tuned the radio. Then out with the fire tin, in with the petrol, brew tin filled with water, and we stood round shivering slightly in the cool air waiting for the sun to come up over the horizon, watching the reddening sky, waiting for the full flood of light before we could light up. The air was crystal clear and cold, our wadi etched with a dark-rimmed silhouette. Other tanks stood out stark in the morning

54

light; other figures stood around their tins. Then over the horizon flooded a warm yellow glow, eating up the shadows, swallowing the tight-drawn outlines. Fires burst forth, lost in the rapidly intensifying light; the tin boiled and we stood around gulping scalding hot tea, fresh and taut and blissful. By the time breakfast was cooking it was hot. Porridge made from crushed biscuit and some form of sweetening, bacon and beans, hard biscuit and gooey sweet jam or marmalade; butter was non-existent and the margarine was nearly always liquid. By then the world was reduced to a glaring shadeless heat and we settled to a pleasant day of nothing.

We talked about the next offensive, our weapons, the latest rumour of a wonder gun, a *Cordon Bleu* lunch or hard biscuits and processed cheese dusted with a fine sprinkling of sand. The flies probed and darted over our uncovered bodies. Sunstroke died in the thirties and we lived hatless, shirtless in shorts and boots. We lived happily in our limbo, very fit and hard, eager, putting aside unpleasant thoughts, professional in our dedication to arms. Like life at sea, story-telling became important and in our wanderings round the tanks clustered in the wadi we absorbed stores of desert experience which mounted into a thorough training. After lunch we repaired into our tank, covered the hatch with an old mosquito net, killed all the flies and prepared to re-read Dingo's copies of an old local papers from Nelson in Lancashire. Then we dozed until the oven in which we squatted began to cool.

The sun ran down its course, the flies went, we donned our shirts and the supply trucks arrived with food, water and stores—perhaps there was mail. We ate our bully stew in comradely groups. In the cool of the evening we gathered round the tank and made one last brew on a petrol stove, tuned the wireless to the BBC and then relaxed into a silent self-supporting family. We unrolled the bedding from the back of the tank, spread it on a tarpaulin beside the tank, took off our boots and socks and crawled into blissful warm blankets, to lie there watching the stars and listening contentedly to occasional firing up at the sharp end, to the drone of aircraft and the occasional crump of shell or mortar. Then we slept. Throughout the night silent characters moved through the rows of tanks, sleepily guarding their comrades, frequently consulting a large pocket watch, waiting for their vigil to end and the moment when they could shake a comrade's shoulder and stir him gently into life. Then a hurried stripping off of clothes and back to the bliss of blankets and gentle senseless sleep.

We left our defensive positions and spread ourselves out on the plateau above, and here we lived for an unrecordable time. Days, weeks and months meant nothing, there was no daily paper, no weekend, no need for a watch—we lived by the sun. The only end was the winning of the war in the desert, so vague a thought that it had no legitimate place in our minds. The next event must be our attack on the Germans. Whilst we lived our existence there was a subtle change as information began to seep down from above. There was an army news sheet, reports of new units and new weapons spread. Above us in the skies we saw the air forces grow in strength, with a consequent diminution of visits from the Luftwaffe. Morale grew steadily and with it an obvious cutback in waste. Privately I wondered how I would face what was to come; a barely emergent force, but one nevertheless ever there, nagging quietly. What happened when face to face and it was him or you? Put the thought aside; it would be resolved when it came.

Suddenly I was told I was due for four days' leave in Cairo, again part of the careful preparation of the army for the test to come. Back to the supply echelon, to the rear echelon, to a small railway station and back through the sand, into the areas of irrigation, past squalid villages and patient buffalo walking round and round their irrigation pumps. And to the great city. Troops coming down handed in their arms at the station and assisted by eager guides found their way to innumerable hotels. To shower copiously, to wear clean clothes, to drink ice-cold beer and eat real food was bliss in itself. I was on my own and quite content to sit and watch life teem by. As I woke sleepily to a sunlit morning a barrel organ in the street outside played 'Annie Laurie', water carts washed down the street and Cairo went on its noisy way. The last night I drank far too much vodka and had my pay book stolen. Before the sun arose I collected my revolver from the station and boarded the dusty, primitive train, back past the squalid villages, the irrigation ditches and the patient buffalo. My eyeballs burned from within from the vodka and from without from the red rising sun.

We were returning from our leave to the battles to come, happily and eagerly. How we should conduct ourselves was a matter deep within our own minds, but we had done all that anyone could ask to date. We had surrendered ourselves body and soul to the army to do with what they might, our remaining task was to continue doing our job when faced with death. Others had managed so why should we fail? It was our unpleasant duty, plain and ungilded. Reared on the cynicism following the First World War we would not allow ourselves any patriotic fervour, Nordic mysticism or bravado. The drain was blocked so we rolled up our sleeves, took a deep breath and plunged our arm in to the limit. We knew we were being exploited by this or that sinister group, we knew that we were led by idiots descended from idiots, we knew that huge profits were being made from our shoddy equipment. We must know this from the barrack room lawyers, and the fighters for the second front, who earned big money in the factories by day and whitewashed walls by night. Deep down inside we knew that it was right and proper that man should be prepared to die for what he considered important. The life of any one of us was so minuscule on the tablets of time that its shortening by two-thirds was utterly unnoticeable. The fact that a man could get up and go out to die a horrible death for what he considered right would live far beyond into the future. A wayside halt, trucks, dusty fly-blown tracks, and back home.

The regiment had moved during my leave to shoot in the guns and was now parked on a flat plateau where we should stay until the off. The first morning I received fourteen days' CB (confined to barracks) for losing my pay book, a not very arduous sentence in the circumstances. Life went on as before, interspersed with very minor events. A truck traversing our area from somewhere to somewhere else dropped a large piece of barrage ballon which I fashioned into a waterproof covering for my bed roll. A Messerschmitt fighter made a forced landing through the tanks and drew up in front of us—the place swarmed with guards so no chance to win anything there.

Quietly and almost surreptitiously during this long period we had all trained in our respective tanks and now was to come to great testing. Composed and knowledgeable sergeants arrived and we were herded into groups for our examination. Simultaneously came a sandstorm, which turned the day to night, reduced visibility to a yard or two and filled every corner of our world and ourselves with stinging dust. Remorselessly we continued with our task until all was recorded and we could creep into our tank, seal it as well as possible, and doze the night away. Reportedly the troop officer was hygienic enough to go beyond the sight of his tank to deal with the calls of nature, and spent twelve wretched hours trying to find his way back.

Now all was complete; we, like all the army, were ready. In this small period the mood had changed from one of chagrined defeat and humiliation to a hard confidence tinged with wonder. Then—miracle of miracles—we paraded and were told the outlines of the battle to come. This was genius. Has any army before been briefed on how the battle was to be fought? Always it has been do this, do that, and don't think. Now we were considered as of sufficient importance to be briefed. Morale rose another couple of inches.

Our primary task was to simulate an attack in the south, drawing the Italian divisions, which were without transport, further into the desert, so that when the breakthrough came further north they would have to be abandoned by the Germans, so causing even greater dissent. General Montgomery's orders were read out and even then his impact was sufficient to coat his stilted cricketing metaphors with acceptance by this highly irreverent bunch of military pirates.

Chapter 6

WE MOVED OFF in the dark, a long winding snake of vehicles each wrapped in its own cloud of dust, each towing empty petrol cans to accentuate the noise and dust and to accentuate the size of the approaching threat. Once inside the tank I was sightless and tied to the wireless by a halter of wire. I had a bucket seat facing rearwards which gave me a good view of the commander's feet as he sat up in the turret and Eddy sitting behind the driver. During the months to come when operating in the tank I saw nothing while on the move, but incessantly the radio droned on and this became my life. I listened to the voices and came to recognise the boredom, the fear, the exasperation, the excitement in the voices I heard. Throughout the regiment we all followed; we heard the contempt in the commander's voice, we all suffered with the bullied, despised the idiot, admired the bold and laughed with the clown. This was my world, hot in the extreme, full of fine blowing dust, noisy, cramped and blind. Should we fight, my job was loading the guns, which almost touched my nose when standing up. However, this was not really on the cards, because being part of the regimental headquarters our task was more executive than aggressive.

The night wore slowly on and dawn found us in position for our foray once dark returned. I turned the wireless off with joy and climbed stiffly out, to eat and relax and wait again. We saw strange faces, new units and listened to the noise of the battle, raging all along the front. We worked up our aggressive instincts firing at German aircraft which were much too preoccupied to bother with some stationary tanks.

Evening drew on and I lay on the ground behind the tank and listened to a first aid party dressing wounded infantrymen coming back from the front. It grew dark and we moved again to the eternal chaos of an advance. The leading tanks ran into trouble in the minefield gaps and we all sat and waited, pitch dark, no lights, confusion, the colonel desperately trying to elicit the facts from scared and harried commanders, who were trying to elicit the facts from harried and scared engineers, who were trying to elicit the facts from the crew of a tank immobilised and shocked by the explosion of a mine. The bangs and crashes round us grew; a shell landed nearby and showered us with debris. Harry's body followed his legs down into the tank and he joined us; I got out some cold coffee and rum and we drank. The rude noises increased, the radio droned on. Now exasperation crept in, an excited uninhibited voice explained how his tank was destroyed.

A grinning irreverent face peered down through the turret hatch enquiring after our health. It was broad daylight and the regiment had pulled back some way during the dark while we all slept. We drove sheepishly back and tried to appear nonchalant. The day dragged on with a steady fall of mortar shells, which achieved little but kept us cooped in the tanks. I climbed out, driven by the calls of nature, took a shovel, scooped myself a hole, cat wise, and went about my business. I debated with myself: was I more moved by physical fear or loss of dignity? Suppose at the crucial moment a flight of mortar bombs came whining over, did I throw myself to the ground? It was academic as I was back in the tank before the next salvo arrived. With the coming of dark we withdrew, our mission complete, and moved up to the centre of the line, where we sat comfortably when all in front was death, torn limbs and the stink of fear. The advance was still going slowly on.

Again we moved forward, this time to exploit the breakout. We parked beside some Aussie gunners, who gave us the news. They were happy because the Japanese advance in New Guinea had been halted. As dusk fell the infantry moved by on their way up, naked and unprotected. A bren carrier full of kit followed them, engine droning, tracks knocking. We moved with the dark; move, halt; move, halt. Through the night we made our way slowly; what sights we passed I do not know. In the darkness of the tank I could hardly see Harry's dusty boots swinging below the turret hatch. In the grey first light I got out to stretch for a brief minute. The ground was beaten and pounded by shellfire and vehicles, there was a lone tank, survivor from another unit. The sun came up and we moved on. Now the light squadrons out in front were in contact with the enemy. The voices on the radio told their own tale. Calm and easy, taut and strained, querulous and demanding. The heat increased and the day wore on and on. Dingo gave me a report on what he saw while I sat blind and grubby, running with sweat and gritty. Night came, and coolness and release from the strings of the radio. With the tanks in close laager we went through the refuelling and maintenance procedures and flopped on our blankets. Sleep, guard, sleep, and we were up and ready to move.

Again the day wore on. At a halt I peered from the driver's hatch in time to see a column of the German 90th light division come rocketing through. All our tanks were firing; before I was pushed aside I saw the turret from a German armoured car go flying with a direct hit.

Prisoners were brought in to join the never-ending stream making their way back. Constantly there were Italians with their suitcases and white flags. Through the heat and dust we moved and fought and moved, until the bliss of night, and the bliss of oblivion.

I awoke cold and miserable to find a steady rain and my blankets sodden. Eddy, Dingo and I collected at the back of the tank to spend the remaining six hours of dark sitting on empty petrol tins under the cover of the engine cowling. We had the greatest difficulty lifting the bedding on to the tank, so heavy was it. We were glad to move off and gain the warmth of the engine. All day it drizzled so that water dripped into the tank and it was necessary to lean constantly one way or the other to avoid new cascades. A German rearguard fought all that day to hold our advance. Field glasses and gun sights were wet and misted, microphones shorted with the wet. The colonel calm and restrained, tried through the bedlam of the air to keep up the momentum. A stray shot hit the ground just in front of us, ricocheted on to the front of the tank which it hit with a great thump and fell into Dingo's lap. So hard was it spinning that his pullover was all shredded at the front. After a minute or two he was quite fit, but months later he was sent home with internal injuries. Again it was dark, but the supply transport was bogged in a morass, and we crawled into sopping blankets to sleep. In the middle of the night we awoke to refuel and refuse cold bully stew.

Again we were off, but this time there was no rain. The sun came out and we halted, tanks and command vehicles spread over a vast area, neatly in formation, and figures standing round them. I sat inside the tank beside my task master the radio. Ginger passed in hot tea, sausages and biscuit. The radio was shut down and I crawled out to the glorious heat of the sun. All around the horizon men were walking out with their shovels to appease the calls of nature. We spread the blankets as best we could and relaxed.

Again we moved and again the transport bogged down—and again the blankets were cold and damp. There was no date, no days of the week, just all day and then oblivion. As I retuned the radio the next morning I picked up a broadcast announcing the allied landings in Algeria and Morocco; shortly after we moved the colonel announced it.

Our great army of vehicles moved as one over a hard travelly plain. A gazelle ran wildly across our path chased by a Dingo scout car. That night I had a warm dry bed and I lay and luxuriated. Never before had I been so comfortable and I recognised the fact, even though we were lying on a bed of pebbles. I knew the meaning of 'relative' and recognised the slavery of comfort.

Now we broke away from the brigade group and made our own way, with Harry performing his duty as navigator. His sole aid was a sun compass, which in fact was the converse of a sundial; if he knew the time he knew our direction. The only trouble was that he did not have a watch, so that regularly at ten-minute intervals all through the long, long day he asked me the time. On the third day in exasperation I suggested that he go and buy a watch. Uproar!

One day, some day, we made contact again with the enemy. The wireless was chattering, and the tanks set off on a mad scramble, bouncing, pitching steeply down. I was blind. There were anguished calls from the colonel for smoke, shooting, bangs and uproar. Slowly order reigned; we were halted and I finally dismounted. We had come down the escarpment on to the coast road beside one of the Italian Albergos and run into a German party drawing out. The colonel's tank stalled in surprise, the 2nd in command hit a mine and so did the MO in his scout car. As I stood, a 3 ton truck went up on a mine and the driver climbed hurriedly out, stumbled a few steps, and collapsed. He had a piece of metal through the jugular vein. As we dealt with this we were violently straffed by some Kittihawks mistaking us for the recent occupants. We flung ourselves down as a roar of flame burst from their shells. Then all was peace again.

We were left with the damaged 2nd in command's tank to await the repair department following up behind. It was time to see what we could win from the debris. There in the MO's scout car was a book—a real book. I seized it eagerly; appropriately it was *The Sun is my Undoing* by Marguerite Steen. This was a wonder, for my reading up to that time had been the labels on tins and Dingo's local papers of six months before. This book was to be a very great joy to me and lasted for months, for the chances of reading were few. I did lose it for a brief spell when we came out of the line for a rest, but found it before we moved again. Alas! The end of the story was gone—presumably to make up for a total deficiency of toilet paper. I have never treasured a book so.

It was pleasant to be free and on our own. We ate in a leisurely way among the refuse left by the armies in their passings. We found some German tinned food, enough water to bath all over and even wash our hair; and some beautiful German tools.

We sat on the tank after lunch, clean, full and gentle. The fitters worked on the damaged suspension. Away in front of us on the coastal escarpment we could see an armoured group advancing. Then we saw two bren carriers coming up on the other side of the road. We saw them making for the minefield and finally we shot at them with the machine gun to try to halt them. The first carrier stopped and his fellow swung round, so neatly to draw up beside him. There was a roar, a black cloud and a body flying up through the air.

I seized the first aid tin and ran over but I was not needed. One of the New Zealanders was with the injured man, his head cradled on his lap. They covered up his legs as I came, legs like those of a rag doll, one at right angles to the body with most of the thigh missing. The injured man was swearing. There was only one man who could swear that way and we had parted in Falmouth when I paid off a ship there three years before. We had been very close. Finally the ambulance came and bore off this tattered remnant of manhood. I went behind the Albergo to be alone. As the afternoon drew on we moved again to rejoin the unit which was by this time stationary at the El Adem airfield outside Tobruk. I began to feel horribly sick and when I went to urinate on arrival I produced a bright yellow stream. Obviously jaundice.

By great good fortune the unit was halted for five days in order to re-equip and I lay beside the tank, feeling like death and unable to eat or drink anything but heavily chlorinated water. I was advised on all hands to go sick, but I knew that once I went back down the line it would be months before I rejoined the unit. On the fifth day I felt quite well and when we moved off again on the sixth day I was feeling better than I have even felt before, with the most devouring hunger. I fairly drooled when preparing biscuit porridge on the following days.

When we moved off the two heavy squadrons had been re-equipped with Sherman tanks and for the first time had parity with the Panzer units, so long dominant. This was a stupendous boost to our morale and we set off in high spirits across country towards El Agheila on the coast, which was the furthest our armies had reached on Wavell's original push against the Italians. To conserve the tanks we were all mounted on vast transporters so that we were only passengers until we caught up and passed through the leading regiment.

There were a few days of pleasant riding with nothing to do and by the time we dismounted and went back to work I was fully fit, but still voracious. We passed through scrubby flat country with very few features. Once we met an armoured car from the leading reconnaissance unit, once we passed by a small fort from the Italian occupation.

Outside El Agheila we met with determined rearguard resistance, but in a sharp day's fighting this withdrew and we moved towards the Tripolitanian border, where we halted to allow the whole support organisation of the army to catch up with the advance. For some time we stayed in the area to deter counter-attack and as a threat. Life was quite peaceful, except for air attacks which the Germans could mount without much fear of retribution, since there were no forward airfields yet cleared of mines and blockages. It was the supply drivers who had a hair-raising time, since they were constantly straffed on the long straight roads on their way up. Our only suffering was from lack of supplies; food was meagre, fuel likewise, and cigarettes and tobacco almost non-existent. At this very juncture, when my pipe was empty, I received a birthday parcel of Burma cheroots, which I had to smoke surreptitiously to avoid too much envy.

The NAAFI truck was dispatched rearwards to buy more supplies and we played 'Sister Mary' daily waiting for its return. As becomes a pirate army the truck was staffed with rogues, on the premise that they would forage better for us than the sober, honest citizen. A group of us, all pipe smokers, formed a co-operative group to share whatever tobacco came our separate ways, for we seldom got any as army issue. The cigarette smokers did better, though in the packets of V cigarettes it was quite common to find a fat maggot in the middle of a cigarette.

Rumour spread that we were to be relieved. It grew and spread until one morning we unloaded all our personal possessions from the tanks and handed them over to alien faces. As we sat on the ground beside them, rather lost and desolate, we thought of them with affection. Our old Honey tank, our home and refuge. In the log book was written 'Condemned U.S. Army 1938. Bought by the British Purchasing Commission 1940'. There was a fault in the electrical system so that the main fuse blew at regular intervals. We had come all the way from the delta by using an empty cartridge case in place of a fuse and taking it out when it got hot enough to smell.

A truck came and bore us and our few possessions off and dumped us at what remained of the rear echelon. We spread out to comb the refuse for anything of value, which was a standard procedure. To our joy we found a large tin of aged margarine, a small sack of rice and an ammunition box full of flour. A bonanza. Some trucks arrived and we piled in and moved off eastwards, in holiday mood.

During the morning we saw a cloud of smoke way ahead and some wag suggested that it might be the NAAFI truck with all our precious tobacco smoking fragrantly beside some unappreciative desert scrub. As we drew abreast of the smoke we saw to our horror that the wag was right. The consensus of opinion was that our gallant canteen crew had flogged all the supplies and then set fire to the truck to hide their cunning. Perhaps we misjudged them, and they certainly redeemed themselves some fortnight later when they had to go down to Tobruk to collect Christmas fare from the NAAFI dump. In order to be first in the queue they slept at night outside the dump beside their truck. The Jerries, with great thoughtfulness, mounted an air raid, which drew the NAAFI staff into their shelters and our desperadoes into the dump to load up what could be won. We ate well at Christmas.

How many days we travelled we didn't count now. At night we would draw into some camp to eat, spread our blankets on the ground and sleep, to rise, wash vaguely, shave in agony, eat and move on again. Our particular truck had a predilection for punctures and we spent the intervals sitting round a petrol fire making pancakes from flour and chlorinated water fried in old margarine. Lovely greasy hot food.

After several days we arrived. That is the truck stopped on a patch of scrubby desert near the sea a few miles west of Tobruk. We climbed off, carrying our blankets and sat on the ground to rest. We ate our food— a mess tin full of tepid bully stew. As we stretched on the ground under a winter sky a light rain spread over us.

The next morning the scrounging parties set out and our rest camp grew: Italian bivi tents, German workshop tents, bits and pieces of junk which successive armies had scrounged from each other. Dingo and I dug ourselves a hole, covered it with bivi sheets, put a ragged fly sheet over it and settled in. We now had a home where we could entertain at night round our cigarette-tin lamp. All around a little scruffy village grew up, dominated by a large German workshop tent as the community centre, a three-ton truck surrounded by cooking pots and cooks, and aloof the orderly room truck with its exalted beings. But someone had stolen my book.

I spent a week sitting in a small hole doing a radio course under the tutelage of Trig, the colonel's operator, and was passed out as competent. I could now rise in the pay scale by a few pennies a day from my basic 2/6d. Slowly we unwound; fear was no longer constantly in our mouths, and we smelt less, not because we washed more, but because our fear had gone. It was surprisingly easy to tell the inhabitants of any dwelling in the fighting areas by their smell, each nation producing its own individual odour.

Christmas Day came and we greeted each other jollily. I wandered off towards the sea, feeling bereft for the first time, but it soon wore off and we had a happy day, a huge feed, and capped it all with a game of rugger on a gravelly pitch, devoid, naturally, of posts. Where did the ball come from in this life we led so remote from the appurtenances of productive man?

Soon the division was on the move again, leaving us resting to the last. A signals section moving up left us to operate a simple field telephone exchange. Naturally the switchboard was practically useless so our only means of calling another unit was to wait until there was a conversation on the line and break in with the request that they make contact for us. Sitting one afternoon, a call came through for an armoured car regiment nearby, but being unable to make contact I suggested that I took down the message and passed it on as soon as possible. I wrote feverishly, checked the message back and sat staring in amazement. I had before me the movement order for the whole of 10 corps; right in the middle was an exact account of our movements. When you come, when you go, when you sit, when you stand, when your very life hangs on orders passed down from the mystic 'Above', you crave always for information, to know what the fates hold in store. Rumour we lived on, but here was I with our exact movements at my fingertips.

My spell on the exchange ended and I made my way to the cookhouse for supper. A dispatch rider stopped and asked me the way to the orderly room, I offered him tea, but he was in a hurry. As we lined up to have our meal ladled into our assorted dishes I passed on the relevant part of the movement order, which covered our immediate doings.

In the orderly room truck the DR handed over his dispatch and waited for a signature. It was nearly time for tea but Sergeant G was a conscientious man, so he opened the packet and scanned the contents, noticing with interest our particular movements. Then locking away the message in the safe he made his way to the cookhouse. He was one of the latecomers so he approached through little groups sitting on the ground eating and drinking. In the queue he was told of our movements over the next few weeks.

Years later we met and through idle reminiscing we learnt the full story. The order was top secret and should never have been passed by phone, so when he heard the orders recounted to him five minutes after he had locked the dispatch away he was disturbed, reported the matter, and an inquiry was held, which tried to establish the leak; but in vain. Had they asked anyone I am sure they would have been able to enlighten them. Fortunately they looked too deep.

Our day came and we picked up our few worldly possessions and made our way to a truck. On the ground I saw my book lying abandoned. I seized it to me and drove off in high good spirits. Behind we left a small and scruffy village, complete and intact.

Ahead was what? Dicing with your life leaves you taut and you long for release. But this soon turns to boredom and so when the order comes to go again there is a certain exhilaration; voices are louder, jokes more bawdy.

The army was still going forward. El Agheila was the limit of our advances to date and now we had broken through and were out into new territory. Up to now every advance had been followed by a retreat so we kept our fingers crossed, but slowly a little thought was growing, that this might be the turning-point, that we might not go back again, that we might advance and

71

advance into some distant land where it all would end.

The advance was earned by the blood of those in front, by the patient infantry, the true heroes of any army, always there whenever things became difficult, and there moreover until they were wounded or killed, going back in for a period and then out for a short rest and in again, knowing that only luck would spare them. The sappers creeping forward at night to lift the mines that blocked the advance, gently probing the ground, so vulnerable to their own carelessness, the cunning of the booby trap or the sweep of the maching gun. The skill and coolness of the gunners dicing with enemy batteries. And our own kith and kin, with our own particular dread, a very real dread of the tank brewing up (catching fire) when hit, so that if you were not wounded you had to move very fast to avoid incineration. We had all seen and smelt the burnt-out tank and seen the charred remnants of a crew.

All these and more on the land and in the air and on the water suffered quietly and competently without question to keep things moving.

Here in this period, an odd anachronism, a part of Britain's ancient heritage played its part. The 51st Highland division, who had played a big part in the advances from the delta, came into their own with the bagpipes.

Imagine the scene. Night has fallen over the bare undulating land. In their slit trenches and fortified positions wait tired but excellent German soldiers. Mortars ranged, machine guns ready with their field of fire marked, riflemen ready, some sleeping, some on watch—prepared, trained, organised and vicious. A slight breeze blows across the desert; a moon filters down, still hazy. Sounds are magnified by the quiet and by nerves, suppressed but not dormant. Suddenly a barrage begins. Soldiers stand-to figurately; in fact they keep their heads down until the barrage lifts˙ and as it does and the small arms start pounding, from around the forward minefields an eerie wailing fills the land. It sinks into the hollows, creeps up the rises until like the moon it is covering everything gently, flowing over all the land. Then the troops advancing, steadily, spread out and almost isolated, feel united by a common bond. Tonight they are not alone, they are one, and they are playing before a home crowd. Inversely the enemy waits, peering into the silvery night, waiting and knowing it is coming slowly, steadily, but coming in its own dour time and leading it will be the bayonet.

The battles that were fought were not great affairs that will fill the history books. Battle honours will be scarce, but to the soldier lying with his shattered leg beside him it didn't much matter that it was shot off in a minor action.

We were happy as we drew our tanks and prepared them. I should have been happier still had I not been gunner operator on the colonel's tank. As the chances of being intimately involved in the fighting were small, this wouldn't solve my problem.

We drew rations for fourteen days and loaded on to vast transporters. As we set off west to catch up the swift-moving advance so began a wonderful ten-day picnic. The awesome presence of the colonel didn't travel with us and each transporter travelled separately, making the best speed it could, and stopping at night where it would. We were in the magic land, the land of the long-range desert group, the land the army had been striving to penetrate since the desert campaigns had opened. We had nothing to do but sit on our tank and watch; to get off and walk when the transporter crawled up a hill; to sit inside the tank and read and smoke when we were bored; and to shout profane epithets at our comrades halted by a puncture in any of the twenty-four wheels of the transporter.

Through the green hilly belt behind Derna we picked mushrooms as the transporter laboured up the hills. We slept at night near a tree, content and happy with our own caravan holiday. Back to the long straight stretches around Agheila, the taped minefields, the odd building with signs warning of booby traps. The elaborate German cemeteries. Gotterdamerung! Burnt-out vehicles and blown roads; a Christmas tree sitting isolated in the sand.

A transporter had gone out of control on the pass down to Benghazi and we were herded into an Italian inn at the top and cooked our chicken stew and mushrooms under a roof. The next day we spent beside the airfield outside Benghazi, a name magical to our ears, where the cloak and dagger boys blew up ships and were blown up in turn. We didn't enjoy our stop there. We didn't like to be congested or near buildings; our home was the wide open spaces where we could keep away from trouble and any point on which the Jerry could range.

On and on, happy to seize this chance before our turn came again. And then it ended. We drew off the road and slowly collected. There was the colonel, and officers and sergeant-majors. And up the road, we assumed, would be fear and a taste in our mouths and the unending boredom and weariness of battle.

We dismounted the tanks and moved off, slowly following the advancing infantry as they made their way through ambush and rearguard actions, blown bridges, fear and frustration, but always the sweet taste of success and the fighting arrogance it embued. Our task was merely to follow to exploit or support in case of counter-attack.

The dynamo on the tank went and we had to run the engine without rest. We moved ten miles forward in the twenty-four hours and used 110 gallons of petrol.

The infantry brigades were leap-frogging each other and the men were finding their way forward as best they could, riding on anything that moved, on trucks and tanks and bulldozers, or just walking on and on.

The pressure never let up and one morning we were loosed. The forward troops were in Tripoli and we pelted down a clear tarmac road in the early morning, sitting not inside the tanks, blind and nervous, but on the turret enjoying the exhilaration. Our eyes ran with the speed and the cold morning air. A great flock of starlings wheeled in the sky. We passed some neat houses and for a moment glanced at a European girl watching elegantly in her house coat. And so we arrived in a field outside Tripoli and stopped and stopped and stopped. There was no petrol and no ammunition and, worse still, no tobacco.

I sat one day on a seat on the seafront in Tripoli and watched some South African engineers trying to replace the broken flag halliards in the high steel posts that ran all along the front. Their ladder was too short so I offered my help in return for some tobacco. I swarmed up the top part of the post, rove off the new halliards and the next day was rewarded with an enormous prize of two whole pounds of tobacco in little cloth bags. I hastened back to our field and summoned our pipe-smoking quartet.

We waited in limbo and then found ourselves engaged in preparing for a victory parade. With no blanco, no brass, or boot polish, there was little we could do but wash our shirts and shorts and try to press them. One set was laid between two planks and spent the night beneath the tracks of a tank.

Our task at the parade was easy because we merely lined the route with our tanks, while the crew stood smartly in front. Being the scruffiest member I was left standing in the turret with a tommy gun as a deterrent to some terrorist. The local inhabitants joined in the fun and were very indignant at being moved off their balconies where, if so minded, they might have been a potential danger. Mr Churchill drove past us in high spirits and waved cheerily to the locals who were now huddled on the pavement. We were proud and pleased, but I felt that I had earned none of this. How many Germans lay dead at my hand in our advance? None. Was I any nearer my answer? No.

A new colonel took over; not a man restrained by the ups and downs of the desert war, conscious of his fears and frustrations, but a successful man from staff, who had to have a field command before further promotion. A man who knew the value of a record, who knew that promotion didn't just come by doing a first-class job, but by letting everyone know you were doing a first-class job.

New brooms sweep clean. A mess tent arrived, a large American car with the colonel's batman, and our tank was removed and replaced with a larger American tank with a crew of five. I was given a wireless set of my own which was tuned to the divisional net, so that the colonel could keep track of all that went on and be better able to advance himself. I'm afraid that this may sound harsh, but as I saw it at close quarters this was my conclusion. This was not geared to advance the regiment, the army, the allies, and so the end of the war. This was a by-product of advancing the man. Nothing wrong in this, only different and sour-tasting to those whose friends lay scattered over thousands of miles of barren scrubland.

So we went back to war again; to hour upon hour with a headset clamped over our ears, which chattered on and on; difficulties, disasters, misunderstandings, stupidity, fear, immense calm. Every facet of the human range *ad nauseam*. Fear again and its taste in our mouths and its smell, dirt, dust, heat and the immense length of the days. The dark soft nights and blissful sleep under the stars; silent lonely guards and rest. But overriding this was a sense of superiority; we were now the better army and would have our will.

We began with a brisk skirmish, in which the fitters' half track captured a troglodite village, the staff car and batman weathered an artillery barrage with numerous holes in the car, and an astonished regiment became accustomed to calls for London Edward Edward Sugar (Lees) to arrive with the staff car to deal with some personal problem. If ever a man earned a medal he did. However, there was a verve and style about what we did, and a few miles less separated the allied armies in North Africa.

I was not happy. I soon found that my job was quite superfluous; only while in action did I monitor reports going through direct to division, and in these periods the colonel was usually far too busy to pay attention to the notes which I passed up to him. So I evolved my own system. I listened to the tactical report made by the RAF reconnaissance planes at first light, made it up into brief messages, and passed them up to the colonel at odd times during the day, while I listened to the BBC.

Now we were in Tunisia and we gave up our occupation currency and carried real Bank of France notes. Indeed the war was moving in our favour. The terrain changed too; no longer the gentle vistas but a more rugged country, with hills and steep wadis, olive trees and more vegetation.

To deal with this a recce troop was formed using Dingo scout cars and immediately my imagination was kindled. To be out in front looking and reporting, to have the sun on my back and to breathe fresh air, however hot and dusty, seemed the height of ambition. I applied for a transfer immediately and spent my days fretting in the colonel's tank. For many this job of mine was a sinecure. It was comparatively safe, easy and not arduous, but inside I had an urge to do more than this.

I had many hours in which to think and I spent much of it trying to create an aggressive attitude to fighting. Up to now I had merely gone along with what came, but knowing a little of what went on I realised that to be any good at this fighting business it was essential to be aggressive, to act aggressively and to think aggressively. None of these things did I do; in fact I had always considered violence as the admission of the lack of reason. And wasn't this to be the age of reason? Only on the rugger field had aggression come naturally to me, and then only in trying to reach the line and not in assaulting my opponents. I found that my daily thoughts affected my outlook and I continued in this practice until I ceased to fight, when I had to start thinking again about reason.

I had great respect for the training we received, but this aspect of war was never touched on nor the chances of being injured. As one of the main dangers of injury is shock, some consideration, knowledge and acceptance of the hazards would have reduced the shock imposed in many cases.

Our forward movement was halted for a while and we held the line with the other arms. Now it was the turn of the Jerry to try his luck, so we suddenly found ourselves as the defenders for a change. But defending from strength and under the cover of dominant air forces, who not only kept us clear from attack but gave us all the tactical information to deal with a typical Rommel thrust. The fighting was fierce and very much to our advantage. At the end of two days we were left in possession of the field and a great litter of German equipment, wrecked and otherwise. I made no contribution to this and the only bother I got into was

78

when I left the tank to urinate. As there was a trapdoor beside me I merely got out and, whilst in the process, an armour-piercing shot sailed near, marked by the flow from its tracer. The tank moved off with me running behind, but fortunately it didn't go very far.

We settled down for a while in order to build up the supply lines, open up forward airfields, and build up for the next breakthrough at the Mareth line. Headquarters troops moved into a little wadi, duly decorated with a couple of German anti-tank guns captured in the rumpus. Our life was easy and relaxed, for apart from stand-to in the morning and guard duty at night, we had very little to do but talk and sleep and cook our corned beef.

One morning I was summoned to act as escort to a Corporal Kelley, arraigned for not being up at stand-to. The whole procedure went according to the book; duty officer, sergeant escort and charged; 'Hats off'; but all with a gentle smile. The punishment was minimal but for me the result was stupendous, for Alf and I became great friends. On our return to England I acted as his best man while his sister acted as bridesmaid. Unfortunately when we were married Alf was still in Germany.

Less cheerful was one of those accidents which upset us, used as we were to death. One of the A squadron crews were doing a thorough maintenance job on their tank. Outside the operator was cleaning the gun mounting while the gunner was working inside on his guns when he fired the 2″ mortar without realising that it was loaded. The bomb hit the operator in the face at point-blank range and he died. These accidents, which happened from time to time, seemed so wasteful and upset everyone. Obviously they should not have happened, but familiarity breeds contempt and overtiredness leads to carelessness.

Our sojourn ended and we moved by night into a

large rugged wadi down which we parked ourselves at intervals. Obviously this was considered to be only a nice gentle holding position, for everywhere beds were being aired, letters written, filthy bodies washed, and a general air of housekeeping was evinced. During the afternoon I sat on top of the tank listening to my damn radio, but with the headphones beside me. I had washed and eaten and was feeling gentle and relaxed. The sun was hot, the air dry and warm, overhead shells whistled lazily back and forth and we blessed our sanctuary.

I sat writing an erotic letter to a girl friend, lost in friendliness and charity to all; the radio droned on with mundane news. Suddenly a report came through from one of the armoured car regiments out in front that they had sighted sixteen Jerry tanks. I abandoned the bedroom scene and scribbled the message down and handed it to the colonel nearby.

Certainly he was aggressive; it was start up the tank, tell the regiment to move at once, and off we went, piling bedding on the back, tying on buckets and fire tins and wiping off soap. A stupefied regiment saw us on the move; desperate wireless operators summoned their crews and like a well-trained and experienced unit they followed, though I have no doubt that it played havoc with the supply of domestic utensils.

As we went the adjutant was passing the news to brigade that we were on our way to see about sixteen German tanks. Brigade passed it to division, who didn't know that we had heard the news on their network, because this was not the proper practice, and took this as confirmation that the tanks did in fact exist.

All in all there was a lot of fruitless activity and coming and going. By dark all was peace again, except that the supply echelon could not find us and we had one of those excruciating sessions on the air trying to guide them to us. The favourite ploy was to fire a burst of machine gun fire in the air because the tracer could be seen from miles away in good conditions. For some reason this was always dubbed with the nomenclature of 'toffee apple'. Why I wouldn't know, except that we always spoke in riddles so that the enemy should learn little from monitoring.

I remember one dreadful evening when we were all dead beat and when the supply group seemed even more mystified than usual. After many toffee apples I heard the colonel, who must have been on his last legs, tell the OC supplies to take a bearing on the North Star and he would do the same and they could establish their relative positions by the difference. A weary and rather diffident voice came back over the air saying that the North Star bore north. There was a silence and a fury of 'toffee apples'.

Once again we were at peace and quiet and this time we had a little hollow with some grass and a tree and I was relieved of my wireless set and given a scout car. Whether this was in recognition of my prompt action in passing some bum information to the colonel I do not know; whatever the reason I was happy. However, the current still ran contrary to my wishes, for I was not part of the recce troop but driver operator in the colonel's scout car. Still this was something; I was moving round, I could see where I was going for the first time since we left Alamein, the sun shone on my back and the air was fresh.

This was my little world. My few belongings were inside, my bedroll on the back, my fire tin and brew tin hung jauntily and there were water cans on either side. I was very happy and the only blot on a perfect outlook was that the syndicate had run out of tobacco again. My only difficulty was over victualling. The tank crews were either four or five, the other scout cars were two and I was one, so that dividing rations was always tedious. I once had to collect an eighth of a tin of milk from seven other vehicles and often had to go from one to another for portions of tins once they had been opened. However, this was a tiny frustration to the joy I cherished in my heart.

We were briefed for the attack on the Mareth line, a defensive position which Rommel had been preparing for some time. There was the usual complication of mixed arms co-ordinating, times of march, attack, order of movement, but the same feeling of belonging to the whole which this briefing gave us. Part of this defensive position was a high bald hill from which the German artillery spotter could control fire with great accuracy. His removal was the task of our friends the Gurkhas, who not only accomplished this at the appointed hour but brought back the spotter's head to confirm their success.

We moved up in the evening just before the light faded, into a valley stuffed with troops and equipment, just as the Luftwaffe flew a sortie with four JU 88s which came in low to a vicious reception of anti-aircraft fire. Within seconds three of the four were flaming earthwards and one of the crew was falling into oblivion on his own. We settled into our little corner and got what sleep we could.

The attack went in without a hitch and the morning saw us moving through the ravaged scene to take up the chase. Lying forlorn and abandoned in the forward defensive positions were sprawled little blue figures: our friends, or should I say enemies of the Italian Folgore division. For the first time I felt the poignancy of their death. This was not a war that really concerned them, but one into which they had been bamboozled. Now, abandoned by their lords and masters the Germans, they lay still and alone, thousands of miles from their warm human homes, from talk and a glass of wine, from their families.

We passed through and saw a tank with a nice neat hole in the front armour made by an anti-tank shell; a neat, smooth hole through four inches of armour plate made as by a warm skewer through butter. Inside the tank where the shell had richocheted round were the bits of the crew.

The recce troop were having a field day. Ostensibly searching out stragglers whom the enemy might have left behind, they were searching through the dugouts for anything they might win. I joined them. We won nothing but some fleas and a curt order to get a move on.

Again we were moving forward, meeting rearguard actions and then moving on. I could see the countryside, watch the tanks moving into action, listen to their chat on the radio, and if finally bored I could read my precious book. I spent many peaceful hours sheltering behind a tank smoking and reading, instead of sitting huddled in a tank, blind to the world outside and bored to distraction. True I was now much more vulnerable to shell fire, for there was no top to the scout car, but this was a small price to pay.

One day during an attack we were joined by some Italians with an enormous 210 mm gun who felt they preferred us to their late allies the Germans. It seemed that the strategy employed at Alamein of making sure that the Italians were left behind in the retreat was paying off. On another occasion I nearly broke my jaw on my pipe when a shell coming from nowhere exploded alongside my car and I shut my mouth hard in fear and surprise.

Often I ferried the colonel when he wanted to spy out the terrain or confer with one of his squadron leaders, and again this let me see more and feel that I was doing something slightly more useful. I had my frustrations, for there was no warning of these excursions, and very often the whole regiment moved off immediately after them, so that I found making time for meals was not easy. The colonel would call his tank on the radio and order his fried bread to be put in now and his tea to be ready; he liked his bread fried very crisp in hot fat. Once back at his tank he could eat fast and then we would all move off. I, on the other hand, had nothing ready and didn't usually have the time to cook, so I took to making up food which I could eat cold, queer culinary masterpieces such as fish cakes made from pilchards and ground-up biscuit which I could keep in a tin under my seat.

I often doubted the validity of our excursions and felt that they were a means to release pent-up energy and strain. One such occasion was on a Whit Sunday; I had promised myself the treat of attending a communion service that morning, a rare enough event, and I well remember my fury at being ordered off on a trip to nowhere at the last minute.

Steadily we pressed on, suffering comparatively few casualties and growing steadily more arrogant and more effective. We came to the next defensive line which barred our entry into Tunisia proper. We stopped again while the necessary forces were assembled, fuel and ammunition piled, and the whole organisation and preparation for the attack on a defensive position was gone through.

Finally, when all was ready, we moved by night to our appointed positions to exploit the breakthrough when it came. As usual we moved by dark with no form of light and in clouds of swirling dust. At the critical points were the odd military policemen with some dim hurricane lamps; as usual it was a case of move and halt, move and halt. At one of these respites I drew up beside a rather flattened jeep parked at right angles to the track. The rather shaken occupants told me that they had pulled off the track and parked peacefully when one of our tanks, wandering a little from its course, had climbed up the back of the jeep, squashed it, and gone on its way while they sat petrified in the front seats.

By morning we were in position, waiting our turn and eating and resting. The day wore on and on and the night came with minimal sleep and the day again. It was comforting to hear the noises up front; they were someone else's agony and we shut our mind to it and rejoiced in our security. In the afternoon the colonel could bear it no longer and I took him off to a crest that looked down on part of the defensive position. Below stretched a completely bare approach, a large anti-tank ditch but scarce a sign of defensive positions.

The back of the ridge bore all the marks of battle: a surface churned by wheels and broken by shells and mortar bombs, bits of wreckage, the smell of fear and of cordite; and the ubiquitous telephone wires which draped almost the whole extent of the North African coast.

A German machine gun was firing fixed bursts at intervals and this took the colonel's fancy. We got on the air to the adjutant, who got on to our artillery troop, who put down a salvo on the estimated position. The shells came whining serenely overhead and landed with a loud crump behind the anti-tank ditch. Sudden angry black puffs of smoke with a vicious red centre spouted from the ground, followed by clouds of dust. Slowly the view cleared and all was quiet. Then the machine gun fired its burst again. And so we went.

The artillery spotter arrived in his tank. The adjutant arrived and a regular artillery duel ensued. Guns trying to remove a machine gun; guns trying to remove each other; unfortunately guns trying to remove us.

I was free now that the colonel had moved to a tank, and I ranged around on foot to see what I might see, occasionally embracing the dust when the whistling of a shell came too near. I came to what must have been a forward dressing station, just a slit cut into the ground into which an ambulance could back, and in which a doctor and his orderlies could work. It still smelt of antiseptic, blood and fear. Somehow it had acquired the incredible aura of fear, pain and near-hysteria; and the endless bored kindness of the medical people who saw this over and over again. I moved away depressed and yet impressed that men bore this not because of some great glory, not because they feared the stigma of the conscientious objector but because they sincerely thought that what they were doing was right.

Further away on a piece of flat ground I found a pack which must have been torn from the side of a truck. Inside were the usual squalid garments and bits and pieces of this vagabond army, and right at the bottom a two-ounce tin of tobacco. I returned to my scout car, elevated and well-pleased with our engagement with the enemy.

The duel was getting quite hectic as the sun began to fade and I settled down for a few minutes with my book. The less the light the fiercer the firing, until with the sun gone from a sky already taking on the tinge of night, and away behind us the first of the stars, a halt was called. A silence fell over the land and troops breathed easy, crawled from their holes, stretched, lit a cigarette and thought about food and the cool of the night. I got orders to follow in the wake of the tanks; I lingered a little to get clear of their shadow of billowing dust. As I moved gently forward I distinctly heard a machine gun fire its fixed burst.

No sooner were we back than it was move again. Obviously the attack had petered out and we were not needed yet. In single file we moved away down a dusty track. In my scout car, following the tanks, I was deluged in fine dust and diesel fumes. Steadily and remorselessly a great weariness spread through my body and I was fighting to stay awake. I sang and banged my head, I sat forward and sat back, but inevitably I dozed and woke desperately to find myself wandering off the track out into the blue. How long the agony lasted I do not know, but eventually and mercifully the tanks pulled off the track on to a patch of desert and formed into laager. I drew up in place and remember switching off the engine and then waking, still in my seat, clammy and stiff, just before sunrise.

I ran over to the colonel's operator to get the codes for the day, and returned to find the colonel waiting to ride at the head of his regiment in the scout car, so that he could find suitable resting place for us all. We wandered off cross country, a pleasant country, rolling and occasionally wooded, but I fell into some confusion when I realised that I had scrambled the code signs and the squadrons were trying to carry out quite unintelligible orders. I was too tired to bother or even to explain the position, but let my leaders sort it out amongst themselves. We parked in a small bowl with a few trees and some half-hearted grass. Now I could sleep and on waking bear my find of tobacco to the syndicate. The attack had not failed completely.

A few days and we were through the line, and no new defensive position lay between us and the American and British of the first army, who had landed the other end of Africa from us. We wound down a hill beside the small town of Gabes and there was a vision of people sitting in their garden in the shade of a tree drinking; then on again in pursuit.

All bunched together, advancing through a gap between some olive trees, we came under fire from further up the hill, and there was a mad scramble for the cover of the trees. Out of the corner of my eye I noticed the scout cars of the recce troop doing as I was doing and sheltering in the flank of a big fat tank, but all was not plain sailing. Before the trees was a bank of earth, a hazard to become common to us from this point on, but unexpected at this moment. The tanks bundled over with a lurch and a jolting crash and no doubt some oaths inside. We had to be very much more circumspect, for should we mismanage we should end with the bottom of the car sitting on the bank and four wheels in the air. A perfect target, it was a case of easing the front wheels up, giving a sharp burst on the accelerator, bellying the car, pitching forward until the front wheels were on the ground and then pulling away. Each car in turn came over faultlessly and then scurried to safety, but it wasn't just the heat that made us sweat.

The squadrons spread out and there was some desultory firing; then nothing. Tanks from the light squadron crept forward and there was no response. We watched one move slowly up the hill to a small wood; he disappeared from view; we waited. After a while the squadron leader called him up on the radio and there was no reply. Night fell and we laagered where we were; an unease filled us all. The light was grey when we moved again and it was damp and cold to our ill-clad bodies. In the wood we found the tank abandoned, beside it was a hand. On the back of the tank were some morphia tablets and near-by a body. The rest of the crew were gone.

All day we moved with an occasional skirmish, the light squadron and the scout cars fanning out in front with the heavy squadrons waiting just behind. Once we rushed through and round a Bedu encampment; a camel hobbled by the front legs capered away and chickens ran in all directions.

We stopped with the light and slept, thick with dust, eyes, nose and mouth thickly caked. I struggled with the maintenance of the car and found the oil bath air filter absolutely solid. Then I slept and dreamt of hands and horrors and woke bemused and irritable.

Again we moved, empty and weary but willing. My old tank commander, Harry the navigator, was told to join me and lead the regiment for five miles on a compass course. He was a stickler for his job and we moved carefully, constantly checking the accuracy of our course. I watched the mileometer and we announced the completion of the course and looked round in relief at a job well done. There were no tanks behind us. The plan had been changed. We made our way back to the starting point and drew up within hailing distance of the colonel. He swung one leg over the turret of his tank and I swore profanely. A shell landed very close, the leg withdrew and the tank took off over the brow of a hill. I filled my pipe slowly. The tank came back, turned hard so that the fire tin and brew tin stood out at right angles, and disappeared in a cloud of dust. We followed slowly, stopped, and made some tea and ate our breakfast.

We were coming into a huge stretch of olive trees, all planted symmetrically, so that in whichever direction you looked you were moving along an avenue between the trees. It was obvious from the radio that the tanks were indeed moving in every direction for a compass was useless when used in a tank. As we ate a leisurely breakfast we listened, fascinated, to the trials and tribulations of the unit, for the Germans were also moving in the same direction through the same trees with the same difficulties so that friend and foe were intermingled.

We moved again, but the car was reluctant now and was using a gallon of oil to each 4 gallons of petrol, so worn was the engine. Eventually we caught up with the colonel who was conferring with the A squadron leader. Obviously Jerry had pulled off to the left and was making for a road which skirted the olive groves.

We set off hell for leather to cut him off. The colonel's tank broke down and he shifted into Harry's, and I dropped Harry to sort out the mess. On we tore, all chaos and confusion; I was laughing out loud at the bewildered messages on the air. Again the colonel's tank faltered and he commandeered the A squadron leader's tank and shot off, followed by the faltering tank. I picked the squadron leader up as he stood there looking bewildered.

Up banks, down gorges, through the avenues until we met a crest looking down on the road. Was it too late? The tanks lined hull down along the crest. Round a bend came a Jerry convoy, rolling happily forward, and then the air was full of shells and machine gun bullets. Vehicles faltered and flamed, men ran for their lives for any cover and the sweaty dust-caked men on the crest— nice decent men—reverted back to their hunter ancestors and gunned down anything that moved. So thin is our veneer.

Some shot kicked up the dust around us as the Jerry tanks belatedly took up the dudgels. There was a scurry to less obvious positions amongst the onlookers. Night fell and we formed up, jubilant, tired and laughing.

First light and a shaken shoulder; boots on, bed roll strapped to the car; start up; nothing happened. I struggled, but in vain. When the regiment moved I remained with Harry as company. We brewed up and had breakfast and then I got to work. There was nothing wrong except that the engine was worn out. Eventually it fired and we moved again. Down below us on the road was the wreckage of the Jerry vehicles, untouched as yet by scavengers. What harm if we saw what we could win?

Below us lay a scatter of vehicles on and off the road, burnt, blasted, on their side or apparently undamaged.

Trucks, half tracks, gun-towing vehicles; the usual odd assortment: German, Italian, American, British. We stopped on the road in the midst of the wreckage.

In front of us was an Arab trying to get a foot out of a boot, a foot now stiff with rigor mortis and devoid of a leg which would have been something to pull on. Around us was carnage. A large half track had burnt with its full complement sitting in their comfortable bench seats, like the passengers in an old-time charabanc. Some lay sprawled and charred, some sat erect and whole as on an ecstatic parade in the fatherland. All were well sprayed with machine gun bullets. At the side lay a torso severed at the waist, scorched and tidied by fire so that it was in no way obscene, but golden and neat like a broken statue. I rummaged delicately in the half track for a pair of field glasses but they were scorched and sticky with the melting fat. We were daunted.

Off to the side was a truck with a large hole in its canvas canopy. We looked through and found it to be a mobile cookhouse, not a truck full of cooking impedimenta such as we used but a real mobile cookhouse complete with range. There were piles of food, tinned and in sacks, and a large side of meat. I hopped in and rummaged about. I threw out tinned food of all sorts, a small sack of tea and then below the meat I found a large sack of sugar, a find more precious than gold. I shifted the meat and it rolled together, disclosing the cook split in two and posing as his own provisions. I tugged the sugar out, pushed it through the hole and dropped out.

Our enthusiasm had gone and we loaded up and made our way, leaving untold pickings, stopping briefly to release some tortoises and white doves which were travelling as pets in a gun limber. Harry was silent on the way up to the unit and apart from a couple of stops beside broken-down tanks to dole out sugar we kept moving. The unit was stopped in a very pleasant glade and preparing for another rest while the supplies caught up. I was silent as I unloaded and made myself at home, but slowly my spirits rose and when Bert came in with his scout car, a very red face, half a gallon of wine and his map upside down I was ready to laugh and joke, but I still don't take sugar.

We were parked in an idyllic spot, or so we thought, a small valley liberally spread with trees. We realised that this was the end of the desert war. No more those endless advances and retreats, the very real hardship which we had taken for granted perforce, the complete isolation from our own kind. All this we knew was now behind us and we could only see the warm green fields and lovely girls. Not the rain and cold and mud, not the restricted visibility, not the bitter lot of the civilians, nor worst of all the breakdown of our comradeship under the stress of greed and desire and a return to a materialist society. So here we rested happy and secretly proud.

Vic took himself off in his rather exhausted scout car to find a workshop that could restore it to some sort of working order. Lean and blond, utterly irreverent, with boots in tatters, shorts too long and half hitched round the waist, no shirt, a peeling nose and an indescribably filthy beret perched on the back of his blond head— combined with a broad Leeds accent and a constant laugh. In our world there were no movement orders directing you to an exact point with some documents to hand in. We worked on a much simpler principle, which was to set out and ask as you went. Vic was sufficient in bedding, water, food and fuel, and though he might make needless journeys if he wanted his car repaired and wanted to rejoin the unit he would manage it. This may seem a very simple solution, but it was one that had proved itself over the thousands of miles of desert fighting, when no depot or workshop stayed put for long and the men up the desert were keen to stay with their units and finish the job.

The army, whether by plan or accident, had evolved a brilliant distillation scheme, which allowed those who had no stomach for fighting to work themselves into base duties all the way from Britain, through the troop ships, base camps, training areas, reinforcement camps, hospitals and the rest, so that those troops in the line, though not enjoying their task, at least thought that it behoved them as citizens to get on with it.

So back to Vic, who also had wandered from his course and arrived at a crossroads somewhere to the north of us, which seemed an unlikely place for a workshop. He drew up before a smart MP and sat waiting happily while a cavalcade of smart scout and armoured cars turned into the road in front of him and made off in the direction in which he was going. The MP waved him on, which is how Vic brought up the rear of Monty's victory parade through Sous.

All holidays come to an end; our colonel left, having successfully carried out his duties, and was borne away by a faithful London Edward Edward Sugar in a rather battered staff car. He was replaced by a young, serious and very professional soldier, devoid of messes and batmen, whom I shall designate Col. C. Also, to my intense disgust, was a Major P, who was assigned to my car until he should take over as second in command. Our first meeting was when he told me to take his bedroll and fasten it on the car. I resented his whole attitude and pondered whether to decline, but discretion bid me obey him. However, I never forgave him for assuming that I was there to do his chores. I knew that I was there, a civilian in fancy dress, to fight what I felt was a necessary war. When we moved I no longer drove blithely about, but had perforce to go decorously, awaiting orders.

The country was now much more rugged and, in fact, never again did we have the tank country of the desert, so that only for short intervals did the tank reign supreme. Most of the fighting was done by the infantry with support from the slower infantry tanks, while we moved in support and ready for any opening which might occur.

This involved me in many journeys with Col. C, because he had to know the terrain over which we might have to act. I enjoyed moving about and I liked him in spite of a seemingly stern exterior. My only difficulty was that he had a slight stammer, and when driving on tracks and cross country, I was sometimes past a turning before he had told me which way to go. I did my bit from then on by looking for a nod or shake of the head and we made our way around amicably.

In the few minor skirmishes which we fought under him, he was quiet and very much in control, and a great confidence grew. He was a great stickler for orders being obeyed, particularly punctuality. The time of march was the time at which we would move and not some vague assessment, and once or twice when he was kept waiting at brigade conferences his brow was dark, and at times he apologised to the whole regiment, waiting on parade for briefing, for the delay. I made quite a few journeys with Major P, but they were usually to collect foodstuff and not of any military significance.

A major joined us from an American armoured division to see how we worked, and I spent a lot of time with his driver, chewing tobacco and exchanging military gossip; I found it refreshing. Slowly we moved forward until we were right behind a bastion of hills which formed the southern end of the final German defensive positions in Tunisia. There, standing out from the land below, were rugged hills with bare rock sides and castle-like pinnacles. Here the New Zealanders, forgetting the finer points of war, clambered up and like an All Black rugby scrum threw their opponents over the sides to gain possession. We waited for the next move and when it came it startled us. We were to move with the Fourth Indian Division round to join the First British American army for an assault on Tunis and the end of the war.

Somehow I lost P and travelled on my own, amongst the transporter-borne tanks and the old worn-out wheeled vehicles of our own and the Indian div. We were in holiday mood again, moving through strange country with new sights and sounds. The road was often steep and we were reduced to a crawl which set the trucks boiling and the transporters groaning and shuddering as they inched their way forward. Col. C was in his staff car but came over and drove for a while to relieve me and, I have no doubt, work off his spare energy.

Up we went until we were in the area of the battles of the Kasserine pass with hulks bestrewn across the land, burnt and burst and derelict; then through little Arab–French villages to our resting place for the night. And what a resting place; we parked on some level ground next to a ration dump.

When we moved the next day the whole regiment were smoking English cigarettes and tobacco and eating chocolate. We had no qualms about this; we were the vagabond army, where survival was to the strong, and those most in need of something acquired it. Along the desert routes were collected dumps of broken and damaged vehicles for cannibalising for spare parts. A recently arrived unit sent down its fitters to collect some spares. Unwarily they left their truck unattended near the entrance; on their return they found their own vehicle resting on wooden blocks with the wheels removed.

Our second day was a happy one during which we actually passed through a small winding town on the slope of a steep hill and saw people, shops and churches and monuments. So we arrived in holiday mood and spread ourselves over a grass-covered hillside. Unknown to us, wary eyes must have been watching and lips pursing.

Again, as the regiment quietly prepared, mainly it is true by drinking tea and resting, Col. C set out in the scout car to survey the scene. There were obvious and immediate differences. This army resembled far more closely the army which I had left in England and there were notices prohibiting all sorts of incredible things like washing vehicles in a ford. The soldiers seemed to know that they were only soldiers with no will of their own, while we all considered that we were there because we wanted to be. Just to establish this fact I swore at Col. C when I thought he had made a mistake and blamed me.

We met some American soldiers up near the crest of a pine-covered hill in a demi-paradise. I spoke to one newly arrived from the cool, bracing air of the north who complained of the heat and listened to Bing Crosby singing 'White Christmas'. I sat peacefully in the shade of trees while Col. C attended conferences, and finally we were on parade being briefed for this, we hoped, final attack of the North African war.

In the evening as the dusk fell we talked quietly and happily, wandering from group to group and tank to tank. Our conversation was mainly shop, for we could have no plans, we had as yet no future. Scoop, the C squadron leader's operator, was saying that he felt he had come to the end. He was calm and content in himself, he had done what he thought to be his part and if he finished that was it. Down below us on the road the Gurkhas were unloading bren carriers from off the transporters,

96

which had brought them round. Short smiling little men, we went down and laughed with them and loved them as brothers.

Our movement times had been laid down at the briefing to the minute for the leading tank to cross the road and for the final tank to clear the road. We wound our way slowly in single file through the day. At night we moved slowly again: quiet military police, dim hurricane lamps, dust and fear. The attack went in with the coming of light and I watched short black figures moving on the hillside in front of us while I drank tea with a Sikh. We moved through the infantry and slowly on. The tanks met opposition but as the day wore on we were moving faster. As the evening drew in we approached a German field hospital with a vast great red cross laid out on the ground as an air recognition sign.

Overhead a very armada of medium bombers were circling. We realised with horrible clarity that we were the target—and these were British planes. I drove with great urgency and parked in the middle of the red cross, and then it rained bombs, but by then I was sitting under the accelerator pedal praying quietly. There was the usual horrible whistling approach, the roar and shudder and clouds of smoke and dust and an acrid taste, and then all 100 bombers had gone and we came out to look again and take count.

Col. C rang round the squadrons and got a nil return of damage. We rejoiced at our good fortune when the recce troop came up with a casualty; a German hiding from us in a ditch had been wounded and needed succour.

The day was done. We laagered, ate, refuelled and re-stocked with ammunition and stretched ourselves on the ground comfortable in our blankets.

Next morning the regiment slipped into top gear from the start. Listening to the radio the squadrons were eager and confident; there was a sharp engagement and gleeful reports of success. From where I was parked I could just see a few tanks down in a hollow. There was a flash of light, the turret of a tank flew and then smoke and soon the incinerating flame from fuel and cordite. The report soon came over the air; Scoop had been right.

Two days later the padre went back to find and bury the dead, Scoop and the driver, neither of whom had been seen since the shot had struck the tank. Sorting out the charred remains, the padre and his helper divided them into two and buried them with two small crosses carrying details of name, rank and regiment. It wasn't until a few weeks later that we learned that Scoop occupied two graves, for the driver turned up one day. He had staggered from the tank burned and dazed and had been picked up by some unit of the Fourth Indian Division and returned down their hospital line.

The German rearguard broken, we rolled again over a country becoming kinder and easier. The adjutant's tank stopped and refused to go, so Major P and I were told to take over his duties, which were keeping a radio link between the regiment and brigade. I stopped the car, tuned my set to the brigade net and locked it carefully. Now I could switch from one net to the other on my set and P could report our doings to brigade; or so I thought. I was driving through a field of corn when the first difficulty arose and I leant over and put it right. But one difficulty followed another, until with an oath I pushed him aside and did both jobs.

Steadily we rolled through the morning, and midday saw us again in a cornfield with, on a crest overlooking us, the silhouette of what could only be a Tiger tank that dwarfed anything we had yet seen. It sat there, arrogant and careless that we could see it, knowing that it could far outrange our guns.

We watched as the leader of the light squadron crept

carefully and with all the cunning he knew through the corn. A gout of flame burst from our friend on the crest and we watched the A squadron leader making a hasty retreat. But if you can't go forward, go round. By early afternoon we were assaulting the last ridge before Tunis and a heated argument was going on as to who had knocked out a 75 mm anti-tank gun on the ridge. And there we sat. Downhill into Tunis.

We waited for the infantry so that we could enter with them and consolidate. But no infantry came and the colonel's patience began to ebb. An armoured car went by, going down into the town to claim the victory for his regiment. Heated messages were now pouring back to the infantry. The armoured car was reported in difficulties; 'Bloody well serve him right'. I was parked beside the colonel's tank and looking up I could see that he was nearly ready to burst as the hours of daylight were frittered away.

The brigadier came up with a long message of suggested action when we finally did move forward into the town. I started to tell the colonel; he went scarlet in the face, slapped the turret of his tank and replied that he would do what he bloody well liked. I acknowledged receipt of the message to brigade and lit my pipe.

Eventually the infantry came and with the last of the day we moved into Tunis and formed ourselves into fairly tight defensive units while the infantry fanned out. I was considering the chances of brewing a cup of tea, when from behind came the rip roar of a spandau machine gun and a German light truck came flying down the road with a machine gun firing. As it approached our road block a rather casual infantryman lifted his sten gun and squeezed the trigger. The truck veered across the road and, crashing into a wall, burst into flame, watched dispassionately by the infantryman. It was dark now and we brewed our tea and ate with a smell of cooking flesh.

With the beginning of day we were the other side of Tunis moving west to pinch out any opposition in this area. Two cars coming towards us did not stop and were shot up; they were civilians returning to what they thought was safety.

A patrol of the recce troop found an abandoned pay waggon with a fortune in French francs lying by the road. They loaded enough to be comfortable for the duration and carried it for days until the money was declared illegal tender. It wasn't until we landed in Normandy that we found that it was quite legal in France.

Finally we met opposition from a hill crest, and the colonel asked for air support to rub it out. This was refused because the planes were at full stretch, so we took it without air support and were establishing ourselves on the crest when word came through that the planes would be over in twenty minutes. Desperate messages flowed, but there was no reprieve; the planes could not be recalled. We sat and waited. It was time to turn to my book which had occupied my mind so often in times of stress. The noise of planes drew nearer, smoke recognition flares were burnt. I slid down beneath the accelerator pedal again and the ground shook and thundered and eventually there was peace and the dust blew away and we surveyed the damage. No casualties and one tank slightly awry.

And so we came to the final crest commanding the final valley through which ran the final river of our campaign. And here we stopped while the units moving east from Tunis worked their way out to Cape Bon and final German surrender. We sat and ate well, for just over the crest I had stripped a knocked-out German tank of its rations, which included a large tin of Danish butter, sardines from Portugal, and many luxuries not seen by us for many moons.

We were having breakfast gently the next day sitting round our petrol fire when we spied a dishevelled figure wading the river towards us. With a gun we shepherded a young bare-footed German soldier to our fire. We were eating, so he ate with us. He was the member of a tiger tank and the rest of the crew were dead. As we finished our beans and bacon and spread butter thickly on our biscuits he wept quietly and we had sympathy.

Two days later the North African war was over and we each had half a bottle of beer with which to celebrate; not much, but we had the joy. The next day we began to move back and parked on the edge of Tunis to enjoy the fruits of our victory. Rather like children we set out simply to look and enjoy the sights and sounds of what was practically a European city: streets and houses and cafés, girls in dresses, housewives and their husbands, and, to the fathers among us, the joy of seeing children. Quite happily we meandered through the town, asking nothing but to feast quietly on this sight. The town was full of soldiers, mainly British and American. We shouted ribald comments at a tank regiment just moving in. We met a crowd round an American soldier standing in a jeep who was harranguing them. We removed three bottles of brandy from the back of the jeep and made our way back to our field, to the space, quiet and simplicity of our life.

We moved away again, away from *our* town out into the barren countryside; and word went round that we were bound back to the desert and away from the flesh-pots of Tunis. This was a bad thing and the first of several bad things that were done to the division. We were not numbers, we were human, and no human will slave for another indefinitely without some reward and recognition. I expect that we did smell, that we did look wild and scruffy, that some of us might have got roaring

101

drunk, but we would have loved some recognition. To bundle us off to some isolated spot, out of the way until we were next needed, was not a good thing. We parked in a steep wadi shaded by trees and someone found a vat of red wine, so we emptied our water cans and filled up.

One night Alf and I made a vast curry out of South African meat and vegetable stew, washed it down with wine and lay replete and in sympathy while we smoked slowly and soaked up the tranquillity of the night.

We started back on our long road to some point east of Tripoli, where the sand blew and there were flies and miles and miles of nothing; we went gaily and laughing, but not happily. All day we moved slowly in convoy, nose to tail, dust to dust, and in the evening we collected and ate and laughed and drank. Bert and his driver took it in turns to drive. In the morning Bert drove, in the afternoon he drank; in the evening he joined us for supper and kept dropping his flour pancake in the sand and washing it in some greasy washing-up water. Paddy was travelling in a luxury coach which the spare crews had commandeered and regaled us with his soft Irish brogue. Vic carried a white hen in his car in the space in which there should have been a radio. It lived in fear of its life, for it was constantly reminded that if it did not lay eggs it would end as stew. Once it flew out and miles and miles of convoy were halted while Vic chased it back and forth across the road. On the last bend as we came to our destination it laid an egg.

Back, all the way we had come so arduously, past blown culverts, wrecked vehicles, endless signs, through to Tripoli and on again. Down the road we had raced that early morning an age ago, and on to Homs. And here we pulled off the road into a little Eden by the sea. In the date palms back from the shore we parked ourselves; a spot we should have embraced as heaven a few months before, a spot obviously chosen with some considerable care by a colonel who was aware of our hurt. It would do, we would enjoy it, but it was no good. What some one did to us back in Tunis was not good.

Chapter 7

WE SETTLED IN. I drew my bivvy, dug a hole in the sand, rectangular in shape with a platform for a bed and a few nitches cut out for stowing my possessions, pitched the tent over it, and I had a home. Here I could sleep and doze; here I could go when I wanted to be alone; here I could keep my belongings. In this home I was dusted with fine sand as I lay. I wrote scratchy letters because the paper, ink and pen were sandy. Here I lay in the heat of the afternoon and mixed my sweat with the fine sand to make a sticky covering, but it was all mine. Near was a tall date palm upon which I could fasten my mirror when I shaved in the morning and under which I could sit in the shade.

Perhaps the most fundamental change in our lives was that we no longer fed ourselves but marched down to the cookhouse truck for our food three times a day. Like all institutional cooking it was a butt. One of the cooks was cross-eyed, which caused confusion because as you came up to him in the queue you held out your mess tin before it was your turn, thinking he was looking at you, while the man due for refuelling took his mess tin away at the critical moment thinking that he had not been noticed. Many helpings of bully stew went on the sand from this. Our friend also had an old charred stick found in some previous campaign with which he stirred the stew.

We remained alive and well, in spite of their ministrations, but undoubtedly we had less to eat than when we fed ourselves. As the summer wore on lunch became an unpleasant chore. We walked down from whatever duty we were on to the cookhouse truck bearing our mug and mess tin, in our pocket a knife. Into the mess tin went some hard biscuit, some liquid margarine, some gooey fig jam and a piece of processed cheese; into the mug some very indifferent tea. Then we would walk back a hundred yards and sit in the shade of a tree to enjoy the repast, by now coated with a fine dust. As we drank the tea we burst out in a sweat which cooled as it dried.

All this was bearable, provided we could make our own cuppa in the dark of the evening when we lay or sat around talking under the stars. This was our one great luxury, and fortunately we had rations left from those unused when in action. These, supplemented by occasional NAAFI trucks and some surreptitious scrounging, kept us going.

Obviously rumour was rife; our future movements were basic to our life. Also there was still that dream of a shower and clean starched clothes and ice cold beer out of clean glasses. If we couldn't stay around Tunis perhaps we could have leave in the Delta, but this too was denied us. We were not happy. Apparently we could sit here and rot until we might offer up our lives again, in which case transport would be available. This may not be fair, but this was how it struck us. It was reported that our friends the Indians down the road had burnt some armoured cars in protest and had won their point, but this was only rumour.

An effort was made to run a rest camp in Tripoli to which we could go for a few days. Indeed I went, but I didn't enjoy it for it was still all army and we wanted to see something else and to make our own entertainment.

There is no doubt that at this juncture there was a very real rise in socialist feeling engendered by our fellowship, by the sacrifice of our fellows and by a natural dislike of the authority under which we lived. What we didn't realise was that our real enemies were the bureaucrats in the delta and with socialism they merely changed their dress and offices. It would still be necessary to go to the workers' camp for a holiday.

We were young and very fit and laughter was never far from the surface, so we made do and got on with what life offered. There were training courses, vehicles to maintain and bring up to standard, the sea to swim in all the afternoon and we had the most marvellous divisional theatre.

The amphitheatre of Leptis Magna had been restored by the Italians and stood dreaming beside us. Lovely old stone, a proscenium stage in front of pillars, terraces leading down to a deep blue Mediterranean, and all around tall graceful palms. In the warm evenings, with a bright moon flooding in and casting dark shadows on the smooth steps, it was magical. Unfortunately it was too beautiful for some of the concert parties who came our way. All credit to them, but they relied on the vulgar and tawdry and this setting was far too fine. Once Laurence Olivier and Vivien Leigh came and played tantalising snippets from *Gone with the Wind*.

Being British, sport of all sorts soon raised its head, and varied indeed it was. A certain fraternity had acquired fighting cocks and these were put to the test, though I never witnessed their ferocity. Soccer was played and obviously there was a regimental competition, even though we were in the high summer. A cricket team was mobilised. There were swimming sports and, even more wonderful, we had a race meeting with real live horses and a tote.

I imagine that this was mainly the work of the Eighth Armoured Brigade who were a little down the road and had a fair share of ex-cavalry regiments. Whoever was the originator didn't matter to us at all; we enjoyed ourselves immensely. The local Arabs supplied the horses and riders, the only difficulty being that they nearly all wore white robes and so we had no idea of where our horse was lying. The radio vans were called in to form a tote and did a very efficient job, taking in the region of £10,000 during the afternoon.

One day I noticed on orders a request for volunteers for men with experience in sail and some knowledge of navigation, so I immediately applied. Eventually I was marched before the colonel, sitting in the back of the orderly room truck, and made my application in person, only to be told that he would not forward it but that I must soldier on where I was. Deep down inside I accepted this verdict because I felt sure that although men were needed for the caiques running up into the Aegean, and this would have been a blissful life for me, the real job in hand was our entry into Europe and the decimation of the German forces. Not that I personally mattered, but I would be one extra. Whether this had any bearing on the matter I don't know, but very shortly after I was promoted to the dizzy heights of lance corporal, and before we left Homs I had attained the dignity of corporal.

I was always struck throughout my army career at the sheer chance of promotion. In this regiment, which was very professional and highly competent, promotion was slow and difficult, and yet in the training and reinforcement field promotion was often very casual and easy. Later on in the war, when I was doing an officer's job in corporal's uniform at corporal's pay, our depot at Catterick was stuffed with sergeants and sergeant-majors whose greatest task was to walk to the mess.

To our chagrin we had to give up our scout cars to a regiment more in need than we. This was quite a blow for we had all lavished much attention on them and had been most punctilious in maintenance and care. Indeed I had really braved the gods when, out for an exercise with one of the squadrons, I had refused to drive the officer in charge over to a nearby village to buy eggs. Let me be exact, I didn't refuse, but said that I would report the use of the car if he insisted. Of course he didn't, but I stank.

In the place of the scout cars we drew bren carriers, small tracked vehicles, open on top, very lightly armoured, very slow and, we thought, horrible. I was at last assigned to the recce troop but again the currents turned aside just as I was expecting to ground on the shore. I was made operator to the troop leader, which meant sitting further back and directing operations rather than reaching the promised land.

Apart from this I was very happy. The troop leader, B, was young and exceedingly nice, the driver also and the rest of the recce were already my friends. When it was originally formed it was natural that the squadrons could spare their bolshie men easiest, so they formed the nucleus. Of course they weren't in fact bolshie but individuals. Thrown in with this were some regular sergeants, who were men well worth knowing; not the traditional rough sergeant, but men quite gentle, yet with a philosophy which would carry them through anything with a smile, and highly competent to boot.

Every evening at supper we were fed yellow mephacrine tablets against malaria, and most particular they were that we ate them. Like fat cattle who are pampered to the very doors of the slaughterhouse, it was important that if and when we died we should be in good health.

We all felt that the Italian peninsula would be our next call, though there were those who favoured Greece and the south of France. Equally it became apparent that we were not to be involved with the first assaults. We relaxed happily and waited eagerly for the next stage.

Once strung up to the tempo of the line it was difficult to spend long periods away from it without becoming bored and difficult, however pleasant it might be to sleep safe at night and get up to a day that had some certainty.

The Sicilian invasion took place and some of our officers went over to report differences in conditions and tactics. What information filtered back to us seemed mainly concerned with women and drink, though there were hair-raising accounts of close fighting. Sicily was eventually secured while we lay on the beach or drank our tea at night under the stars, and was followed almost immediately by the invasion of the Italian peninsula proper. And still we lay on the beach, relaxed, knowing that our time was near and savouring the remnants of the ease which we had spurned for so long. A landing craft came into the harbour at Homs and we practised unloading ourselves down the scramble nets; a pleasant interlude but not of intrinsic worth, for it is difficult to unload a tank down a scramble net. And then we moved.

We drove the seventy miles to Tripoli and loaded ourselves on to tank-landing craft for our journey to Salerno. The invasion had already gone in and was meeting trouble, though well established ashore. We were obviously part of the follow up. So it was goodbye to North Africa, to all the many races we had fought with and come to know with affection, to the desert which had been home for many of the men for some four years, to the army in which we had fought, and to its spirit and ethos which had done so much to make our task possible.

To many of the more experienced this was an enormous change which they found difficult to encompass, and I truly think that none of us was ever again so much a part of any of the varied armies in which we served.

Facing the quay lay our ship with its loading doors

gaping open. We drove steadily up the ramp and were engulfed in another world. No longer would we be awakened by the squeak of the pulley as the Arabs drew water from the well in the morning; no more the open vista and weirdly changing shapes under the heat of the desert sun; no more the sleeping under great ripe stars; no more the understanding, ribaldry and irreverence of this magnificent army. Forward to Europe obscured by hedge, house, ditch and river, cluttered with people and buildings, isolated by bridges and worse, much worse, deluged with rain, swept with winds and always nearer to the core of the military game where proper dress and correct procedure took preference to killing the enemy. Yet we went with light hearts, for somewhere at the end of all this we could go home. Finished. Released.

We drove through the gaping doors, halted neatly on the lift and were carried to the upper deck where we secured our carrier firmly. The upper deck was loaded with carriers, what was left of the scout cars and some trucks, while below went the tanks. Other squadrons were loaded into other craft and other regiments into further craft—a great mass of organised detail just to move part of one of the many divisions necessary for this further episode in our great game of Cowboys and Indians.

Again we relaxed. Our part was done for the moment and we could rest happily on the laurels of the navy for a few days. Unhappily the laurels were a little awry before we were put ashore, for on board the craft was a jeep, painted blue and lettered RN, which the skipper boasted he had stolen from the army. Some of our drivers, knowing the court martial which must have followed the loss of a vehicle, took the distributor from the jeep and threw it into the sea. When this was finally discovered there were dreadful threats that we should not be put ashore until the culprit was named. This was

110

no great threat and was treated as such.

We sailed out into the smooth blue sea and made our way northward like a crowd of schoolboys on an outing. We lounged on deck and showered ourselves—perhaps for the first time in eighteen months. Our only complaint was that we were still fed on bully and biscuits. With the navy's system of messing it was necessary for the army to feed its own personnel while in transit, and do it with no equipment; a very different story from troops lucky enough to sail on American-manned ships.

I never took kindly to the Royal Navy's arrogance and disdain for the wretched soldier. I had a very high regard for the navy's spirit and competence but even they made their mistakes. With great good sense they had developed the myth of the silent service; their mistakes might remain hidden. I had been at sea, I had sailed in a convoy that must have been wrongly routed, I had seen mistakes made and incompetence. To show disdain for a soldier being put ashore to fight and fight again for months and maybe years under dreadful conditions, was less than worthy of a worthwhile and competent body.

This bothered us not at all. At the time the sun shone, the sea was smooth and our little trip was in every way idyllic. As we came up towards Salerno there was a cargo boat wallowing and low in the water, davits swung out and lifeboats away. My stomach turned quietly over at the recollection, but how much pleasanter than in the grey cold heaving wastes of the North Atlantic.

As we came up towards the landing beaches there was all eagerness and pointing arms, the epitome of a cross-channel steamer in August.

To our vehicles; engines roared into life and ran until warm, then all was still. From the shore was the thump of guns; overhead a fighter roared amidst the insistent banging from the anti-aircraft guns. The ship was vibrating throughout now as she made her run into the beach. The stern anchor went down with a clatter and we felt her shudder as she took the ground and surged sluggishly on. A slight jolt and we had arrived. Ahead were months of fear and laughter and death. Some were on the list for maiming, some for easy wounds, some for death. But for everyone it was a case of renewing their resolve to accept what was in store and to push quietly and remorselessly forward. This army needed no bullying from the rear, no sadistic police to drive it forward, no machine guns trained on the backs of advancing men. This was a civilian army coming to grips with what it rightly took to be the enemy. There was no glory, but if the luck held there would be a pint of beer in the local at the end of a day's work.

The first tank rolled out and shed a track. So the vaunted Desert Rats arrived. Eventually we were disembarked and went without incident to our allotted area. The initial troops had done us proud. We had room to live and sleep in peace, but from the wreckage the deed had not been easy. Wrecked equipment strewed the area, happily much bore the evil black cross.

Evening came and in accordance with our recent training we put on slacks, rolled down our sleeves, wiped ourselves with mosquito cream and ate mephacrine tablets. How the tiny mosquito must have laughed; he achieved so much that the juggernauts of war could never achieve. As we stood around our evening fires watching the cooking of our meal we came out in blisters of sweat which remained trapped by the cream. That very first evening we began to realise how we should miss our lovely desert.

Waiting for our turn for the line we explored our new surroundings. Fields dense with crops blocked any view, dead bodies lay undiscovered amongst the tall tobacco plants, arms and ammunition amongst the tomatoes. All was lush and voluptuous, fat and greedy, soon to decay, to rot, to stink. Too much, too much; unlike the fine bare aesthetic sands of North Africa. Nearby a pretty river ran fast between steep banks, to which I went with some hand grenades to fish for supper, but the catch was small and thin. We gorged on fruit and fresh tomatoes and at night stood in beads of creamy sweat around the cooking pots.

We were to take the line. Assembled altogether we went through the ritual of briefing which had meant so much to us since its inception. Briefly and precisely our roll was enumerated: background, objectives, methods and details of movement.

With the coming of the morning light we were winding our long snake-like way to the north to await the breakout by the infantry. To us the sights were strange. Gone were all the old unit signs, the accustomed equipment, the very landscape, for not only were we in Italy, but we were now part of the Fifth American Army. However, the basis of war did not change. All day we straggled forward, stopping, waiting, moving a little and stopping again. Once we halted near some abandoned cottages with their furnishings spread abroad in front. I hopped out of the carrier, picked up an umbrella; 'you never know it might come in handy'. Night found us sleeping beside our tanks stretched down the road, and tomorrow the road was all ours. We had been too long at it to fret now; what would happen would happen. Before the light of day our fires were flaming beneath the brew tins and another campaign began for us.

It was all the same again but quite different, for now we couldn't see, now we were often restricted to roads, and above all else there were civilians whose fate often lay in our hands; civilians who welcomed us ecstatically

113

with flowers and grapes and walnuts, so that by the end of the first day the tanks were decorated like hearses, the linkage was jammed with walnuts, and the crews were sticky with grapes. It was all very exhausting, for we could no longer fight our war away from the eyes of strangers but now we must do it on the open stage.

As we came into small villages we had to gain in stature, the liberating heroes, big calm men, fearless and competent, going about our business quietly and without fuss. As we drove out again we shrunk to our normal diminutive size, no longer the Western heroes but very ordinary mortals playing a real game for very high stakes.

The following day saw us bogged down in a slogging match with a very determined rearguard. The area was dense with vegetation, thickened by the habit in this part of suspending the grape vines from wires strung between high poles, which effectively blocked any area of vision. B had parked the carrier beside the HQ troop so our only danger came from persistent mortaring and shelling, but the tanks were having a rough time adapting to the new circumstances.

Ginger came back speechless at the German whom he claimed had grinned at him down the barrel of his gun. One of the tanks came back with its sergeant dead from the shrapnel of a shell which had struck the side of a house. We lifted him out and laid him on the ground for the doctor. Limp and floppy, there were holes in his beret and white plaster on his eyelashes. I helped the doctor for a while as I had nothing to do except wait for the next salvo.

A troop of the Rifle Brigade set out to give close infantry support but were decimated by a mortar barrage laid down presumably by a well-concealed spotter.

Steadily we made ground as one strongpoint after

another gave. Late in the afternoon we went off in the carrier to link up with the people on our left. Winding through the thickly covered terrain I was standing in the back with the bren gun cocked and ready, surprisingly unafraid. We came to the outskirts of a town and down the street. Little bundles of clothing lying still marked the wretched civilians somehow involved. I entered this in my book of hate, for no doubt a passing German truck had sprayed them with a machine gun for fun. A dead dog lay quietly in the road and there beyond was a tank from our friends. So we passed the first day of our new term. From then on it would all be easier.

We advanced steadily and met a new hazard; it rained without ceasing all day. We got wet but this was of no real consequence since what mattered was that maps were sodden even under their plastic covers, field glasses were misty and useless and, much much worse, our microphones shorted out and wireless communication, on which we depended for an ordered and controlled advance, ceased substantially to work. I raised my umbrella and sat dry and ordered.

When next we rested I was asked by the colonel to procure him an umbrella and shortly afterwards they were a common article of armoured warfare. Some considerable time later on the battlefields of Normandy I saw a tank advancing crowned by an umbrella with an air recognition star painted on the top. I like to think that this was my contribution to the efficiency of the British army. Certainly I am sure that an umbrella was essential to the proper fighting of our tanks in rainy weather.

Now we had got our rhythm again and the advance went well. The recce troop, because it was really well used, proved of great value, which was a source of joy and pride to us.

Sergeant G had a broad grin, infinite courage and an unbeatable philosophy, and was winding his way in his scout car through the narrow lanes and creeping into villages. In spite of his frantic gestures, he was constantly being carried shoulder high round the square by the liberated Italians cheering and singing. Jerry, of course, with the range recorded, was only waiting for the noise of rejoicing to loose his mortar shells and as often as not Sergeant G was dropped as the populace ran for shelter. Sergeant H, more dour, but no less effective crept up a bridge in his car and dropped the front wheels over the edge of a crater blown in the crest and spent an unhappy night facing a machine gun. The carriers, too, were grinding their slow way across the soft ploughed ground and praying that there was not an anti-tank gun in that clump of trees. Vic, the irreverent bricklayer from Leeds, regarded Lt. E, his commander, as a bit of a nit and a pansy. Remonstrating with him one day about driving so gaily down a small valley, he was quietly informed that there were snipe feeding at the bottom by the stream and that they wouldn't be there if there were men about. Vic was generous about his mistake.

The real work was done quietly and without fuss by the tanks, all of us acutely sure that we were directed by a man who knew what he was doing and really cared for us. There was a touch of autumn in the air which tingled in our northern blood.

I had a poisoned hand which festered and grew sore until my arm was puffy like a feather pillow and I felt sick and bloated. At night I went to see the doctor who travelled with us in his armoured half track. He fed me some tablets and put my arm in a sling but there was no thought of being sent out of the line. He was tired and it was the end of a long day when emotions were stretched to the limit and weariness welled through us all. A head appeared at the door of the half track and announced that it had piles. 'Good God, so has everyone else!' shouted the doctor, and the head withdrew.

116

The next day wore on and on and my energy ebbed with the power in the batteries of my wireless. We sat for what seemed hours in the shade of a huge building surrounded by ammunition dumps and demolition charges. Wires led into piles of bombs and crawled up the walls like ivy and were fed into the building. The world was flat and dreary. I strained ever harder to hear and then apathy overtook me and the batteries died.

There was a great palaver that night about bringing up fresh batteries when all I wanted was to lie down and sleep. I didn't want rations and fuel and ammunition or damned batteries—but have them I must. Eventually the endless day finished and in the morning I felt new again. In front was the Volturno river and we could do no more.

We came thankfully out of the line for a rest and to wait for the poor long-suffering infantry to cross the river and establish us on the other side. We spread ourselves between the grape vines which were festooned from tree to tree, sat on the grass, and enjoyed the cool of the autumn. Beneath a tree a young Italian sang a catchy tune as he picked walnuts. I listened with pleasure and watched his grace. He sang 'Lili Marlene' and this was the first time I had heard it, though I read later that it had been a favourite with the desert troops. Our sort of desert troop had had no radio on which to hear it.

And then it rained and our grass turned to mud. We huddled under the shelter of tarpaulins stretched from the side of the tanks and lay on the boggy ground. The colonel refused permission for the officers to bring up their messes on the ground that the troops must put up with these conditions, and so it behoved them to. He certainly took his share of the mud and ate the rough food with his crew.

The recce troop found itself a barn and we moved in. Part barn, part farmhouse with a fireplace, at night we sat around a blazing fire and all came out with colds. We went to the local town and bought what was left of their strong drink. That night we drank beautiful precious Strega out of enamel mugs and it ran down our throats like molten gold, smooth and burning and cinnamon. I leant against a bren carrier for support when on guard duty and laid my tommy gun to rest. The world was full of golden stars and I wasn't safe with a gun.

We became thoroughly idle and did not rise for stand-to at dawn, but lay warm and snug in our domestic bliss. One morning as we lay there the colonel walked past the door, stopped, looked in and addressed our OC, who by then was standing in his short shirt tails trying to look composed. When we moved to some old barracks nearby we all had to rise an hour before stand-to.

We crossed the Volturno and fought our way slowly on. There seemed endless rivers, streams and dykes which frustrated our advances. Jerry was as thorough as ever and made us earn our advance with here a tank and there a man. In a wood, soft and open, with one of a tank crew lying waiting for the ambulance. Round faced and gentle, zoo keeper of a gorilla in civvy street, face burnt, lips raw, still quiet and unperturbed. Knocked out for the second time in a week he had dragged the wounded from the tank. Sitting eating in a grassy field when suddenly the burst of a shell from a high-velocity gun, the shell beating the sound of its coming. A first aid box, the ambulance, back to corned beef and biscuits.

Another halt but this time there was sun. We sat round the carrier having breakfast, Captain B in his wicker chair that we had found, discussing the value of drill. A quick shave and then act as escort to a trooper charged with not being up for stand-to. A horrible occasion when we were all on parade for identification for a case of attempted rape. Standing in our lines while a frightened woman walked between her stern-looking bodyguard of officers, she stops and cowers, cries out in fear and points. A man is led away, a decent man, quiet and conscientious but fond of drink; far from home, near to death, emotions on edge and now this. No glorious return, proud and happy; all he had won torn from him. I felt rather sick and humble and sad.

The cold and wet returned and I was tired, not just physically tired but drained and weary. Chalky told of having typhoid while working in Cairo and of how he had to lie quite still for four weeks. I dreamed of the bliss of not being allowed to move, of having to lie still in a clean bed. The thought of catching typhoid was an ecstasy which I enjoyed for some time.

A rumour spread and grew and somehow it rang true. As I walked across the rough ground the coins in my pockets jangled like the clickety-click of a train. Was this an omen? We were going home! They actually told us.

One more minor advance. Bert found a bridge undamaged over the Garigliano and no one would believe him so he came back and brewed tea until he was wounded by a mortar bomb. We settled down in reserve and suffered the coming of winter. My sheepskin waistcoat which I had bought in Libya stank in the damp. Shaving in the cold of the morning became a misery as the razor rasped over a stiff beard. We lay beneath our tarpaulin and waited. It rained and there was mud but we could suffer this. Recce parties mapped the paths and tracks for those who were to follow.

Then one night we drove out. Moving through the darkness of the night, grinding slowly, we felt our way. In the back of the carrier next to the engine it was scorching hot so I stood up. My top froze and my bottom baked. The driver swore at supply vehicles coming forward with their lights on so that he could see nothing.

And then we were out, out of the line, out of the war.

119

We slept in a school under the luxury of a roof with a clean, hard floor for a bed. The next day I felt as if I were dying with an aching chest and painful breathing, but it was a very minor chill and gone in twenty-four hours. We did what we could to the vehicles in maintenance and cleaning, and handed them over to a Canadian unit horrified at the old wrecks that were to be theirs. With the carrier we passed on a magnificent set of tools won from the allied and enemy armies over a period, and even more important a large ammunition box of thick brown sugar.

We were borne away southwards to Castelemare, a little town to the south of Naples which looked across the bay to Capri and upwards to the smoke plume of Vesuvius. Here we found a home in a spaghetti factory and settled ourselves in to await a ship.

Here all about us were the fruits of civilisation and we were ready to taste them, but apart from the utter joys of a hot bath in the Romanesque public baths, we found that we were out of touch with the material world and were usually happier with our own company and our dreams of the future. Not concrete dreams of reality but that warm bottomless dream of a future.

Now we had to learn how to be soldiers, how to drill and march and shout orders, how to put on equipment and clean boots so that we could join the army at home which had been suffering these horrors unendingly until they too could escape to foreign shores and the battle-field. There were sergeant majors and messes and a whole mystic world about which most of us knew nothing.

A new major arrived in battledress and bright shoulder flashes, he-man boots and a knobbly cane. We looked in wonder and were a little frightened. We knew the capabilities of the German army and had the very greatest regard for it, but what was this? We knew that the German army would never reduce us to tears, and we

120

knew that the British army had done so many times. Was this some phantom sent to destroy us before we ever got home?

One night the phantom arrived outside the guardroom, one time the weigh-bridge office at the entrance to the factory, and commanded the astonished sentry to turn out the guard. Being a man of resource the sentry blinked his eyes and called 'turn out the guard'. The phantom and the guard awaited a rush of men hastily pulling on their equipment. Nothing happened. Together they called for the guard and again nothing happened. Then with stentorian voices they demanded the guard, and again nothing happened. For a second time they joined in demanding the guard, whereupon the door to the little building opened part way and a tousled and sleepy head appeared. 'For Christ's sake shut up,' it said, 'we're trying to get some sleep.' Then the door shut. Soon after that the phantom left for worthier fields.

Our life was simple in our bare whitewashed rooms, now devoid of spaghetti machinery. We slept in rows on the floor at right angles to the wall. Some had made themselves low beds from old boards and a few bricks; many preferred the concrete. Our belongings were in our big and small packs neatly ranged behind us, our equipment hung from nails driven into the mortar between the bricks. We washed and shaved in the open at troughs and tore at a hard stubble with blunt blades, ate meals from our cookhouse, and went through the charade of being soldiers.

We held debates and discussions, mainly in the field of post-war Britain and mainly socialist in content. One I remember now, and one which has had very considerable bearing on my life, was on education. On the subject of education the independent schools came well to the fore, and the colonel inveighed heavily against the snobbishness of the normal preparatory school. Admiring him immensely and valuing his opinions, I decided some years later, when I was running a prep. school, to abhor any taint of snobbishness, with unfortunate results.

We met the locals and made friends, but they were so poor and had so little that we found it difficult to accept hospitality. We did find a house where we could eat spaghetti napolitan and sing Italian songs round the piano with our hosts. We drank wine in moderation or not, according to temperament. One of our characters arrived home one night so far gone that he gnawed the corner of the wall behind him and left the imprint of his teeth in the whitewash. We visited Pompeii and toured the ruins. We visited Naples in search of anything to buy, but either there was nothing or the price was exorbitant.

We squirmed at the desperate hunger of many of the people and their incredible poverty. Yet they were gracious and gay and sang when the sun shone from a blue sky and the spiral of Vesuvius melted gently into the clear, clean sky. Cars and lorries carried large iron stove-like contrivances at the rear to produce gas in place of petrol.

Sometimes we marched in file through the steep valleys surrounding us, drank from the cold depths of wells and rested in the shade of whitewashed peasant houses. Then the world was beautiful and we forgot the fighting again and were warm and ourselves. We watched the sea for ships, swapped rumours and stuffed our packs with lemons and our minds with dreams.

Loaded into trucks we were moved to some barrack places in Naples and waited. Authority became harassed and tempers became shorter, but we had been in the army long enough to be able to wait indefinite periods. This time no one wanted to be late.

Again we loaded into trucks, to the docks, and on board a troop ship. A troop deck, overcrowded, short of air, cluttered with equipment and games of cards and everlasting boat drills, dogged by a life jacket either in the way or frantically lost. We were happy; we could eat and sleep, no mud, no guard duties and gently a form of peace was creeping through our bones. Our officers joked with us and let us know that they esteemed us. We could all hate the OC troops who dogged us with ever more elaborate drills, with chalk lines in alleyways saying 'blown up'. The messengers ran hither and yon in a game of marine snakes and ladders and we grew steadily more unco-operative.

On Christmas eve we docked in Oran and spent Christmas day there before taking off again for the last leg home. By then we had settled into our separate groups: the talkers, the sleepers, the know-alls, and the desperate card players, who were winning and losing months of pay which they had not even drawn. At night I took my blankets on deck, still wrapped in my piece of balloon fabric, and slept amid the rushing wind, warm and fresh.

One grey evening our ship moved slowly up the Clyde. We didn't want to wave or cheer, just to savour this land of ours quietly. For me it was a bare two years since I had sailed down the very same river, but many faces had left these shores before the outbreak of the war. Some had left newly-affianced girl-friends, some were coming back to vacant places round the fire. At that juncture we were all happy with our quiet dreams.

Chapter 8

IT WAS DARK and damp and the ship was still. We stood around quietly and content, there was no need to rush, to announce our presence, to make desperate attempts to phone. Time was now on our side. After two or three or four years away, why spoil the savour for the sake of a few more hours or even days? We were sure of ourselves with an inner calm that was often taken as conceit, but was a very different thing. We had mainly come to terms with our life and with the many faces of death. Somehow somewhere inside we had a knowledge denied to those who had not lived this life, intangible yet firm.

There seemed no need for enthusiasm and histrionics. We took unkindly to learning new techniques, for we all knew that death was the lot of everyone of us, whether in the near future or in our old age. Truly the regiment was tired, yet like an old war horse at the smell of powder it raised its head and would not be left behind. Being human we wanted it both ways.

Eventually we disembarked and loaded ourselves and our meagre kit into trains—meagre kit because we had all left belongings at the base in Egypt. Astonishingly enough these caught up with us about a year later, and when finally I opened my kit bag I was amused to find that I had set out to the battlefield with a copy of *The Importance of Living* by Ling Yutang.

We sat in our train and dozed. I thought back to the

night journey on our way out to the Middle East, when unsure and insecure in our ignorance we craved action of some sort, seized on scraps of rumour and bandied second-hand tales. Now we dozed as the train wound its slow way through the dark. A story had passed through the train that Norfolk was to be our destination, which had not pleased us overmuch. We yearned an easy billet in some lush and easy area.

With the first grey glints of a winter day we collected a mug of tea and some food on the platform on Essendine station and then we were on again unappeased. The tea was thin and only warm, the food featureless. Tired but docile we left our carriages at Brandon in Norfolk and were carried by truck out into the countryside, rather bare and grey under the winter sky, into the pine plantations around winding roads. And we had arrived. A small road ran along the side of a small wooded hill set out with nissen huts.

We made ourselves at home in a bare hut; wooden beds with hard mattress, a stone floor and in the middle a round stove. There was a meal awaiting us in the mess room, but the tea was still thin and the air was cold and sank slowly into us.

We were a small unit in the recce troop and we took up two huts. We knew each other, we relied on each other, and we were resourceful, so that soon the hut had a homely air, the stove was red and our ration of coal for the week was rapidly disappearing up the chimney.

We were to grow fond of our camp and as the spring spread slowly over the land it was beautiful; but when we ventured forth that first morning to face the bleak English winter we saw little to please us. There was a NAAFI canteen housed in a nissen hut down at one end, which sold beer and blanco and filthy tea in an atmosphere of soulless boredom. It was a place seldom visited except by those who had to drink beer. In a little

125

glade on the way we met some red squirrels capering together and saluted them and thanked them for their welcome.

Leave was the great topic and to this end the administration worked unceasingly and without respite. Faced with a world of forms and indents and strange procedures, they fought manfully on until we all had our leave passes and trains to match them, ration cards, clothing and, most important of all, our money. This on its own must have been a mammoth task for I, who had been away a bare two years and was on the princely pay of four shillings odd a day, had some £70 to collect and count with clumsy fingers. But it was done.

Once again the trucks took us to Brandon station and eager-faced we reached the platform. I asked an indifferent porter if there were any newspapers and got a very sharp reply. I smarted under this and decided that the less said the better. I knew that I should be welcomed at home.

When we finally reached Peterborough it was late on a cold winter night and there were six hours to wait. Like all wartime stations it was full of homeless vagrants in uniform, both male and female, bearing resignedly the cold bare discomfort as a necessity. The waiting room was full and cold, but a few fencing stakes soon kindled the coal we had removed from the tender of a train and we spent a gay night, leaving shortly before the dawn to journey northward.

At Grantham six of us got out and piled our packs in a heap while we fought for a cup of tea; packs so different from the khaki of the home-based troops, for these were bleached almost white with the desert sun and were quite innocent of any blanco. When we came to reclaim them mine was gone—the beautiful German field glasses which I had won in Italy, the small presents which I had scraped together, removed by some obscene hero. I boarded my train swearing in a histrionic fashion, much to the amazement of some American airmen.

Somehow this homecoming was going wrong. All I wanted now was to get home, to the warmth and love, to the acceptance, to fill the empty chair. At Nottingham I had to change stations and I walked out into the station yard and stood still. Everything was so drab with the strain of war. In the middle were a group of American servicemen with local girls hanging round their necks. It was all horribly tawdry. This was no stupid jealousy but just sorrow. We had lived with the thought of the dignity and warmth of Britain and we desperately wanted to be part of it again, but here we were strangers in a strange land.

I caught the local train and assuaged my heart as we stopped at little stations down the line, stations called in unintelligible English, still some gardens, oil lamps, fields and beasts grazing. And so I came home to my people, to a place where I belonged, to the country and its simplicity.

There were coal fires and oil lamps, gracious trees and unkempt lawns and the quiet rhythm of wartime life in the country. The lemons which I managed to bring back were raffled at whist drives in the neighbourhood. The chemist dug out a precious badger-hair shaving brush from some dark recess to replenish my needs. Just to be at home was golden. There was no high life and no desire for it. We were not heroes and we knew that there was more to come, so it was a case of savouring to the full all those things which we realised were so dear to us.

Refreshed I went down to London to act as best man at Alfred's wedding, one of many put into cold store by the division's long stay overseas. There was a synthetic air of gaiety about London which rang no bell with me, and apart from one night with Alfred drinking and talking quietly and enjoying our ease, I did not like it.

Somewhere deep down inside I had not found anything very special to live for until I went to the wedding and met Alfred's sister, and then life took on a new meaning and I have no doubt gave me the incentive to stay alive in the months to come.

So it was back to Brandon station in the bitter cold on a train packed to the doors with an ever-changing horde of servicemen, now grown apathetic at this nomadic life which left them shivering in unlit, unheated stations all over the country.

We boarded a truck in the early hours of the morning, which slid off the road a few miles away and wrapped itself round a telegraph post, leaving us bruised and bloody to walk some six or seven miles back to camp. Around 4.30 in the morning we found ourselves passing an airbase and made for the cookhouse where WAAFs plied us with hot, sweet tea and bacon sandwiches before we went on our way.

Life in the camp was pleasant and our duties, apart from keeping warm, were few as we had no vehicles. Officers left and were replaced with new ones, men went on courses, weddings were discussed and we grew used to the three-and-a-half-mile walk either way to the pub in the evening. Our hut was happy and we got away during the weekends fairly regularly. A way of life developed. The regiment ran rugger and hockey teams which played neighbouring units, giving us some real exercise and allowing us to work off some of our frustrations.

We found the local population singularly unattractive and unresponsive, just when, more than anything else, we all craved to be made at home. No doubt the people were as tired of the war as we were and had seen too many troops pass through, but they seemed very happy to welcome the many Americans who were stationed in the airfields all around. But then they had more money.

The longer we stayed the more hostility grew. We formed our own community and every time we saw some tank damage we smiled with pleasure.

The winter wore on and we began to collect our vehicles, new Stewart tanks from a factory near Hatfield where they were prepared after arrival from America. This was a gay trip and it was nice to be able to say thank you to the people who painstakingly prepared the vehicles and never saw them again. They were good tanks for reconnaissance and a great advance on the earlier versions which we had used in the desert.

The new Humber scout cars we condemned as soon as we saw them: too little armour, poor across country and a driving position which was almost impossible to leave in a hurry. Where were our beloved Dingos? Then the first of the Cromwell tanks arrived. This was the crunch for this was to be the strength of the unit. There was gloom.

I will always remember a vehicle recognition class taken by our OC in which we questioned him about thickness of armour, weight of projectile and muzzle velocity of the respective tanks, ours and the Germans. He was an honest man and when he had finished there was silence. Each sat quietly brooding. Again we were to be hopelessly outgunned, and, after our brief period of equality, this was a bitter blow.

No doubt many reasons can be given for this, but we knew that many of us would die because the tanks lacked a proper gun. The experts who brought the Cromwells were no help for they insisted that all was well and that we knew nothing. What could be done was done to improve matters. Like the scout cars the driver could not get out with any alacrity and to men who had watched their friends incinerated this was depressing. New hatches were devised and fitted.

Training started and the sun began to shine. We spent

hours on schemes in the surrounding countryside and found it lovely. With this return to activity spirits rose and in the recce troop we were happy. I received letters that mattered and life was important. Easter came with hot sunshine, wives visited their husbands, Bert got married locally and one or two tanks managed to act as escort on their way to an exercise. One gorgeous spring evening Joan and I got engaged.

The war went on without us, and yet like everyone in Britain its sights and sounds were obvious. By day the American air force circled endlessly, forming up into greater and greater groups, filling the clear winter sky with vapour trails which blotted out the pale sun. Late in the day back they came, some limping along low down with one or more engines stopped. We looked and had some understanding.

As we walked to the pub in the falling dusk, low down over the fields came the hordes of British night bombers, not in formation but scattered and unceasing. We drank and laughed in the warmth of the pub and walked back to a warm hut and the understanding of friends. Sometimes in the early hours, when the world was chill and cold, we would stir at the throb of returning aircraft and we were humble and thankful. We read of our friends in Italy bogged in mud and cold with the chill of the mountains and realised that we had no worries.

I did make one great advance, for I was given command of a tank and would no longer be tied to the OC, who sensibly was more occupied with commanding his troop by radio than doing his own reconnaissance. I had a really good crew. Flash the driver was a regular, thoroughly competent, unflappable and prepared to accept with equanimity whatever came his way. Chalky was operator gunner and had been in the recce troop almost since its inception. And the lap gunner was a young cockney.

Our troop leader was a new young officer who was exceptionally nice and quite unsuited to the task. We spent days exercising with him and trying to teach him something, but to very little avail. Quite how he had got to this point I do not know and I felt really sorry for him. Fortunately, after a short time in action he was posted to some other task, thus undoubtedly saving his life and that of others, for he was nothing if not brave. I met him later on in Europe and he told me that he realised that he was hopeless in this particular job and we laughed about it together.

Shortly before we left England Chalky was removed from me and given a tank of his own, and I acquired a new operator who was quite useless in the field. I felt that now I had the chance to discover what it felt like to be virtually face to face with an adversary.

The OC came one Saturday and told us to prepare two tanks to go down to Felixstowe to give some landing craft practice. When were we coming back? We weren't!

So the time was coming again. Hurriedly we sent telegrams to those who had slid off for the weekend and were needed. The rest of us pretended to be twice the number and B pretended to be taken in.

We motored down through the early summer sunshine and established ourselves under the lean-to of a school, where we could sleep without fear from the rain. Our bed of asphalt contrasted strangely with the foyer of the local cinema, with its opulent carpet with foam beneath, but we were comfortable enough and thoroughly enjoyed the change and our rides round the bay in a landing craft.

After a few days, with our mission complete, we made our way to Orwell Park where the armoured end of the division was collecting. This was a fine house set in lovely grounds sloping down to the Orwell, and was in happier times a prep school. Spread through the trees were nissen huts in which we lived. In the middle of the cricket ground were more nissen huts and the main building was some sort of administrative centre. In the evenings nightingales sang in the trees and the honeysuckle was coming into bloom and filling the roads with fragrance. Once established, we moved off for the weekend before the main party arrived. I spent a glorious day and a half with Joan.

Each vehicle was issued with a waterproofing kit, and we worked in the sun sealing cracks and seams with tapes and making the vehicles thoroughly able to wade through water below turret level. This was our first introduction to Bostick, and we finished each evening covered in sticky black, which we washed away with petrol. We were happy with our work, the brooding was over and once more we were moving—and this time for the final fling. In the evenings we went into Ipswich and drank and relaxed, often sleeping there to return on an early train in the morning.

Whitsun came with glorious weather and we were confined to camp. We sat on the sunken wall and watched the local people making the best of the weather and a brief holiday. Except that we could not go to the pub there were no complaints. There was almost an air of gaiety and relief.

We drove out of Orwell Park and down the road to Felixstowe, where we parked our vehicles nose to tail and came back by truck to sleep. The road outside the gate was churned into deep ruts by the tanks turning sharply as they came out. Next day in sunshine we joined our vehicles and made our slow way to the docks. Now people waved and brought cups of tea, and sadly we thought that they only waved when we were going.

In the docks was a money-changing van issuing Bank of France notes such as we had thrown away in Tunisia. E still had a 5000 franc note as a souvenir. Once more we rolled up the ramp into the dark interior of a landing ship.

Out in the river the ships lay moored two by two; identical ships, some American-manned, some British-manned. At breakfast the next morning the queues on the two ships came from opposite sides of the galleys, so that as I stepped out on to the deck with a tray covered with food from the American galley, a friend stepped from the British galley with a meagre little breakfast. We had unlimited coffee all day, and in exchange for a bottle of whisky I got a mound of milk and sugar, which would be of far more joy to us.

We sailed down channel in convoy and hung around off the west country, and then we turned south and in company with a vast stream of ships of every conceivable size, shape and use we steamed steadily towards our destination.

Where that was we did not know; all we had been given was a suitcase with maps for the whole of Western Europe. What did it matter provided it brought the end nearer, for now there was some point in there being an end.

Time passed and we compared our happy circumstances to those in the small landing craft who were cold and wet and often sick. Aircraft passed constantly over us. We were briefed on our job and point of arrival and told that the invasion of Normandy had begun, a fact we accepted without comment since attacks were always beginning and this one was just one more. At night we were almost halted and we could hear firing from the shore and the assembled naval craft. There was the rumble of bombing and occasionally the sky was lit with tracer spraying upward like some giant firework.

With the grey of the morning we gazed in fascination at the vast throng of craft assembled off the beaches and the orderly way in which they were moving. Apart from shrimp boats and sailing dinghies I don't think that there was any sort of craft missing and there were a great number of entirely new concepts.

Around noon we grounded in the shallow water, the ramp was dropped and we made our way one by one through the water to the beach, leaving behind another ship scrubbed and garnered so that no trace of our tenancy was left.

We came up the beach following our appointed track, through some soft sand, past a tank damaged by a mine. I thought of all the trouble which had gone into getting it there; the years of training, the hopes and preparation, all gone in one vast bang. Lying beside it was a broken whisky bottle.

Up the road and away from the sea, our journey was far more relaxed than most motorists returning from their day beside the sea. There was a brief glimpse of fortifications and damaged buildings and we were winding through the small, gentle country roads. Already there were unit and directional signs put there by the Geordies who were making our entry so comfortable. Already on a small wooden cross the local people had put some flowers. Some miles on we turned into an orchard and parked. The war had started again. Would I now discover what I hunted?

Chapter 9

So we stood poised again for the conflict, but subtly this was not quite the unit it had been. The remorseless pressure which it had suffered, the softening of a few months at home, and finally and most important the realisation that the tanks we were to use were not a match for the German machines, had had its effect.

On top of this there was a feeling that because we had done well in the past this was no reason that we should be expected to continue to carry the burden now. In fact there were too many men who had done enough to warrant an easier passage and there were enough of us who had not suffered the same burden who could have carried the torch. This is all hindsight, and the decisions made were no doubt made with all the reason and information available at the time.

The next afternoon we moved, and kept moving for several days to cover gaps and suspected counter moves. It was strange to be on the mainland of Europe, for to us Italy had been an extension of the African campaign, and there were advantages. One day while out on patrol we came to a deserted farm with a German vehicle outside. While investigating we found 32 eggs which we gratefully acquired and in repayment we moved all the animals which were tethered outside in the fields and had each eaten a patch quite bare of grass. That night we cooked the eggs in our pan which would just hold eight eggs, this being each man's ration.

We worked with the infantry for a while, but the closeness of the terrain and the stiffening resistance made progress difficult. Somehow there was a mood of frustration and it was with joy that we were routed round to the south to try to exploit a gap which the Americans had found down towards Caumont. Stopping for a meal in a field we found a box of cigars which some German must have dropped and we smoked our meal break away in luxury. Astride the Caumont road I was sent to make contact with the Americans on our right, and I parked the tank up a narrow tree-covered track while I went on foot to locate our friends. Within a few minutes an allied fighter bomber was over our lair and let go his stick of bombs; such was the grip which they held over the battlefields. I found the American infantry digging in and looking very competent indeed.

As we moved out of laager before it was properly light, and did not come back until it was dark, one of the great troubles was lack of sleep. Our hours for rest were reduced to something like four, of which time had to be given to refuelling, loading ammunition, dividing up rations and doing a guard duty. The agony of dividing compo ration boxes each for fourteen men between tank crews of four and scout car crews of two, when dead tired, cannot be imagined.

With the first grey light of day the guards around the laager shook bundles hidden thankfully in their blankets. Figures arose silently, rolled their bedding and strapped it to the tank. Engines roared into life and radio sets crackled. No one spoke; no one needed to speak, they knew their job and it was too early. Each clasped a mantle of silence to him. It was enough to do what was necessary without having to abandon your own self to the common pool.

Bodies and minds were tired and ahead lay another long, long day and perhaps an everlasting sleep. Speech could wait until later. We moved away to our appointed duties.

I found my friends of the Hussars, introduced myself to my opposite number and prepared for a day of liaison, a day of endless listening to the doings of the regiment, which I must pass to him while he did ditto. Hours and hours of listening and perhaps something might happen, perhaps we could add two useful sentences to the whole.

The division attacked down the spine of the high ground that led eastwards towards Villers Bocage, one regiment leading, the others fanning out to keep the flanks clear. The fine morning air cleared our heads and a smoke induced a feeling of life. By four o'clock we were in place and ready, mentally and physically prepared for the day ahead.

From odd snatches on the radio we realised that the advance was moving well and then no more; we dealt with our own problems. The sun was warm now and I looked at my watch. It was only half past eight and we seemed to have been out all day. Flash, my driver, leant back in his seat and smoked and dozed. Occasionally he leant through his hatch and produced some food from the ration box bolted to the front wing. Midday came and I was drooping. The radio droned on—colonel to squadron leader, troop leader to his C tank, recce troop, C squadron, B squadron, troop leader to squadron leader, brigade says—terse and controlled, each taking a minimum of time, for the radio was our life blood. One loquacious report could hold up dozens of pieces of information.

Slowly things went wrong. Captain B must have bought it by the request and counter request for the doctor. Our friend of the snipe was in trouble. Nothing dramatic, just a request for the ambulance; the passing reference to Charlie 3 Baker going. I stayed and passed my messages and reported back, and miraculously the day began to end.

Towards evening I was recalled and put out on the flank to watch. Chalky met me and told me about the death of B and E. Vic was wounded and had gone. On the far slope of the valley we watched a German tank move slowly parallel to us and then stop. Our peashooter would be worse than useless and the big boys were playing their own game on the southern flank where Jerry was making his appearance. Obviously the artillery would enjoy dropping a small 'stomp' on top of this lot. I looked at the map, I looked at the ground, but somehow my mind refused to work. I couldn't come up with a perfectly simple map reference. I called Chalky and together we sat in the evening sunshine in front of our protecting hedge, warmed and gentle in the evening, trying together to do what should have taken part of a minute. Eventually we gave up and some lucky Germans walked contentedly through the Normandy meadows as the evening drew on and the shadows lengthened.

On the other flank things had hotted up and we had had one or two successes. In each troop there was one tank with a powerful gun and they were able to knock out a German tank at reasonable range. Naturally Jerry very soon tumbled to this and they were always the first on his list when given any options.

News trickled back. The leading regiment, meeting a Panzer division on its way up to the front lying in ambush, had run into real trouble and had been nicely decimated. Regiment two was sitting dangerously tight while Jerry was making his way down the flanks. Here a German tank, there some infantry, more shelling.

Chalky and I sat in the shelter of our hedge and watched. Someone was reporting a man moving towards him. Was it a civilian? Perhaps it was! No, it wasn't! It must be a German infantryman. Suddenly the

138

colonel's voice, with a touch of weariness and exasperation, 'Besa the bugger then', a besa being a machine gun. We were all refreshed; we knew what to do and were back in reality.

The radio told too many stories from the pitch of the voice, the constant appeal for directions, the vacillations, and they were catching.

As dusk drew on we closed up a little with tanks in pairs facing either way to deal with infiltrating infantry. It grew dark and we formed up near the road ready to draw out when our leading units had passed through on our inglorious way back. As we pulled out on to the road the heavy bombers were streaming overhead to add their weight to the destruction of Villers Bocage.

Slowly we made our way in the darkness and with the first light of the next day we drew into our respective fields, threw our bedding on the dewy grass, crawled inside and slept. We woke, performed our duties and slept, but somehow the more we slept the more tired we got. We had no officers now in the recce troop, and UJ came from one of the squadrons to take over. Quietly we grieved B and E, for they had shared our beginnings and we theirs.

I went out to guard a ford over a stream one night. We drew up in a little valley beside a small farmhouse, which was being evacuated with the help of some infantrymen. The farmer came across to us with a bucket of rich yellow milk which was covered in thick cream by the morning. We were left alone in this quiet warm valley with our farm and stream and rich grass and the evening was gentle, but the night was long and dark and the butt of the machine gun was hard and brutal.

On another day we guarded a ford over a stream, but here we could play the Roman for there were a flock of geese grazing to do the watching for us.

Lying on the grass one day watching planes circling

139

idly in the high blue sky and the puffs of anti-aircraft shells bursting harmlessly, the two coincided and a flaming meteor fell earthwards. Only then did we think of the men in the planes.

We were all on parade one day for the colonel to address us. He was leaving to become a brigadier and hadn't wanted this, but these were orders. There was considerable emotion on both sides. Obviously he was desperately proud of his regiment, in which there was a great store of admiration and infinite trust in return. However, this had to be.

With a new colonel and a new OC we moved back nearer the coast into an area of tight little fields and great high hedges and here we stayed for some time. I was given a troop and E's tank which had had the turret removed to make it lower for reconnaissance. I didn't regret the turret from the safety angle but I did regret its removal when it rained, which it did with some regularity. We carried out a fairly intensive re-training scheme to get used to a totally new type of terrain, but the recce troop spent the greater part of its time driving round the innumerable new tracks which the engineers created constantly, so that we were familiar with the whole terrain.

I left England with high hopes of enjoying the French countryside but here there were so many units, so many men, that it was hard to feel the land around. In the next field there had been a battery of medium guns who had left behind bags of cordite, which looked for all the world like uncooked spaghetti, and when given wings from the waterproofing plastic still sticking to our tanks, became diminutive flying bombs which we flew around the nearby meadows.

As we left our field we had to pass two knocked-out tanks of a sister unit as grisly reminders. Often we would go to the little crossroad village of Jerusalem

140

where lurked a vast Tiger tank, knocked out in the very early days. It was illuminating to sit up on the turret and look down the vast length of its huge gun. We believed the tale of the leading regiment of our brigade who were ambushed in a cutting beyond Villers Bocage. A Tiger tank had come over the top of the cutting and knocked out the first and last vehicles. The commander had then appeared from his turret, taken off his hat and bowed to the remainder. Such was the feeling of immunity given by this great gun and weight of armour.

A summer evening in July, a warm sun still shining, the day's work done, in the distance the sounds of war. We were sprawled about on the grass, or cooking the evening meal, smoking, talking, enjoying the luxury of being alive and being free. In a group sat some men playing cards in front of a tank. In the lap gunner's seat a man sat reading, his head showing through the hatch. Idly his hand dropped to its normal resting place on the butt of the machine gun; idly his finger found the trigger and squeezed. One small bang, a wisp of smoke from the barrel, and a card player rolled over dead, shot through the head. The reader lay on his face and sobbed uncontrollably all the evening through. In the morning, in the clear innocent morning sun, we lowered a limp blanket-clad shape into a small hole, said a few halting words and gently filled the hole with soil. Even now death could make us catch our breath.

Talking with a friend from B squadron, I enquired idly after X, an officer for whom we had very little use. This meant in fact that we felt he was no good at his job, for to us the ability to fight well was synonymous with the ability to end the war and remain alive—the only two important considerations.

X had died. His tank had been hit and had brewed or burned. My friend, not far distant, saw that no one escaped. Slowly the smoke had risen from the open turret of X's tank, mixed with haze from the heat, and gently drifted upwards to be caught by the breeze. Back down the radio went the message 'Able 5 is brewing'. The battle went on.

Some time later my friend, looking towards X, was stricken with horror. Slowly, wanderingly, a blackened thing showed, nodding, groping blindly upwards through the hatch, unable to recognise it or seize it. Only a frantic courage and persistence could achieve this.

A sergeant from another tank climbed on to the back of X's tank and had his leg shot off by a waiting panzer. Other men went to his help, but by the time the panzer was removed poor X had gone. I was humble in my judgements. I knew that at least X had answered the one question which dominated so many of us. We had yet to resolve our problems, but to get all the answers meant reaching the very end.

Being a troop leader I now was able to read army intelligence reports, which were amusing and gruesome by turns. They included an authenticated report of Russian prisoners of war, held in conditions of starvation by the Germans, buying the flesh of their own dead comrades in their canteen. And the wonderful tale of the Blighty company, which caused Jerry to prepare against poison gas or germ warfare. A loquacious British prisoner had referred to the Blighty company (this was the heavy mortar company), which was well back behind the unit because of its range and in consequence was considered to be almost at home. Some quick-witted interpreter had caught on to the word and connotated it with blight, germs and gas.

We had a new colonel, gaps had been filled or improvised, and everyone was eager to be on with the job. Fighting a war on the threshold of Europe and a stone's throw from England was horrible. No longer could we get quietly on with the job, governed by the dictates of war, but now there was a constant pressure brought by the hordes of journalists, politicians and hangers-on which distorted the job. To ask men to go and die is accepted as reasonable if a country feels itself seriously threatened, but to ask them to die in public is nothing short of barbaric.

We did not really consider ourselves as part of the homeland but as expatriates with our roots buried along the path which the war had led us. I think we all remembered with some bitterness our time recently spent in Britain and the smiles and waving when we were leaving again.

Finally we were to move and we lay down thankfully to a last night's sleep sheltered by the high hedges, but Jerry, who had other ideas because of an airfield nearly constructed next door, took the opportunity to give the area in general a pasting with his artillery. There was nothing better to do than to lie there in our blankets dozing, waking every time something landed near. In consequence we were rather jaded when we moved the next day and there were some gaps in the crews.

Slowly, because of the density of the traffic, we made our way towards the east, and by dusk I had reported to a sister regiment once again to do liaison. The sun had gone when I arrived and a plane soaring high in the still sky let rip with a machine gun at a fire left burning too long. No harm was done and indeed, apart from a few oaths at the miscreant, little notice was taken, for a swarm of hornets had taken the opportunity to spread alarm among the nearby tank crews.

Moving in the dark of the early morning we made our way up to the start line—a long roaring snake of armoured vehicles, dim red hurricane lamps, impassive military police, control vehicles parked beside the road with wireless sets burbling. Over the narrow Bailey bridge and it was growing light.

With the day came a host of heavy bombers, not in formation but at varying heights and apparently travelling singly, yet so well co-ordinated that they fused over the target into a huge and ever-changing mass. We watched astonished as it rained bombs, changing subtly from dark solid high explosives to a glittering rain of incendiaries. Then they were gone, making their way quietly, superbly organised, into the wings, and we began a slow crawl forward.

I followed my opposite number blindly. I could only listen to my own regiment who were behind us and knew not what my friends were doing. We stopped on a small plain crowded with every type of army vehicle, indeed the only thing missing from this mass was the Co-op bread van. Incredibly a tank in front of us was hit by an AP shell and the crew stumbled out. If there were enemy guns in range they could not miss.

For some time we all sat and waited and then we found our way ahead again, over a railway line and into a field of wheat standing strong and healthy. Coming through it was an airman, who had been shot down, marching a group of German prisoners back towards the rear. We moved well for a little, until we came to another flat stretch littered with knocked-out Cromwell tanks extending right away to the ridge in front.

Delay, frustration, ignorance of what was happening. We made our way across to the left down into a wooded valley and we were passing Canadian troops all wearing shell dressings under the camouflage nets which covered their tin hats. The day had been easy for us as we came up a rise into the open again. Some shells landed nearby; violent black smoke with a brilliant red centre and large jagged pieces of metal tearing at the unwary. The tank I was following stopped and the commander jumped down swearing. The driver, who had his head out, was hit. I got the lead from his headphones under his arms and we tugged him through the small hatch opening, floppy and inert. Our hands were wet with blood; we laid him on the ground; from his head oozed blood and sticky brains; he quivered and made quacking noises, and then mercifully died. The officer was crying.

On again through the slow long day. The fighting was fiercer now. Forewarned, Flash removed his head inside the tank and drove with his periscope; crossing a bank this went too. The hole left by the removal of the turret gaped open and we felt horribly vulnerable, yet how secure compared to the infantry.

Towards evening I was parked at the corner of a field behind the crest of a hill from which a lively tank battle was being fought. With only a machine gun I could do nothing. Down in the ditch below us lay a wounded German, part of a mortar crew. I gave him water and a smile and took his map case and instruments. I heard on the radio Jack reporting that he had just taken the surrender of an artillery battery from its colonel.

The light was going slowly and the air warm. I sat on the top of the tank as we ate cold rice pudding from a tin. I looked at my hands gory with dried blood and brains. Nearby two flail tanks were talking on their radios and coming through on my set. The commanders were tired and their nerves were frayed. I could hear the scorn in the voice of A and the almost pleading voice of B as he complained bitterly that A had 'pissed off without warning'. It was frightening to hear men so open in their dislike on the one hand and dependence on the other.

UJ came up on the air, asking my position and then querying my reference. I too was frayed, so I asked if he thought I couldn't read a map or didn't know where I was.

Across the valley three German tanks were brewing, the flames flickering in the half light. It was dark and we pulled into laager. I bedded down with my friends, and we were excused guard duty.

I woke in the cold morning hours fleetingly to a bombing raid. A little to our left there seemed to be some trouble but I only recollected this the next day as something seen in a misty dream.

With the light of day we moved onto the forward slope of the hill. Below, our two regiments were fanned out. I watched an SP gun sidle down through the fields and start firing into A squadron below us. As so often happened, my report was ignored or disbelieved, so I had to smile wanly when the squadron called for an ambulance for their squadron leader.

Some time during the morning the Germans broke off the engagement and we moved cautiously forward. Going down the hill I knew that there was a God and a life hereafter and the whole bloody business lost its sting. Dying was no longer very important—but the fear of pain did not diminish.

By early afternoon we were parked in a tiny hamlet, while the squadrons probed slowly forward. This was not a good place to wait, for it was of course well-documented by the German artillery and mortar crews, so that I spent a most uncomfortable afternoon going from one tank to the other with messages and further information. Once some rocket-firing fighters straffed us and I was wrapped round the back of a turret.

Our two regiments, advancing on parallel courses, began a battle. It wasn't wise to wait until recognition was certain and once the firing started it was difficult to stop. As usual it was some time before anyone would believe what I was saying, but being able to listen to both regiments I knew what was happening.

One of our leading troops was engaged with tanks on its right. The officers' tank was knocked out, the troop sergeant went to pieces and chaos reigned for some minutes with the colonel desperately trying to elicit what was happening. Suddenly up spoke the calm assured voice of the sergeant's radio operator and thereafter he ran the remnants of the troop. Within days he was a troop sergeant; within weeks he was desperately wounded by a mine; and within months he was discharged with a 100 per cent disability pension and returned straightaway to full-time teaching.

Two of my crew were now useless with fear and Flash and I had the added burden of being doubly cheerful. We hadn't time for pity and I am glad that we hadn't the inclination for scorn.

Marching solidly through the village went an infantry company—slow obvious steps, no hurry, no eagerness, no fear. A bevy of shells fell and with them one man, now with one leg. His comrade behind stopped and bent over him and then straightening up undid his gas cape from off his pack and spread it over the peaceful figure. Quietly, and with barely any disturbance to their movement, they had passed through the village.

The pressure on the air diminished and my scrambling backwards and forwards between the two tanks became less frenzied. It grew dark and cold and we laagered in a field, desperately tired. We forwent any food and once fuel and ammunition were replenished we slept, oblivious of the past day and the one to come.

But the dawning day brought the sun and a halt in our ever slowing advance. With the sun warm on our backs and nothing really to do we relaxed. A leisurely breakfast, a wash and shave, straighten out the tank, make the necessary calls both on the air and to nature, and I set out on foot to explore. I was very impressed with the way the Germans had dug in and prepared themselves against air attack and air burst shells. Lying beside a track was a long, lean, raw-boned German, sprawled dead, his uniform tight over his muscular buttocks, the soles of his jack boots facing me. I raised him with the idea of taking his pay book for intelligence purposes, but he had no face, only a waving sea of maggots.

In the late afternoon my friends advised me that they were withdrawing and that the infantry were taking over. I passed this back with the request to return, but the colonel, only hearing the second part, told me to remain where I was. So remain I did, sitting one solitary tank alone and forlorn with the infantry holding the line. Around ten o'clock I called again and asked what I was to do. This time I was given a map reference and told to come back. Perhaps there are still soldiers sitting alone in the fields of Normandy.

Finding a field by a map reference on the superb maps which we used was not difficult, but it would have been very much easier if we had been able to use a torch with which to read the map, instead of my scarce supply of matches. Eventually out of the black loomed the solid shapes of some tanks. Some brief words with a sentry and we found a space and slept where we sat.

As a resting place our situation was not ideal, for the cornfield, or one-time cornfield, in which we were parked was a sodden boggy mess on the forward face of a slope which was within artillery range of Jerry. There was no future in trying to sleep in the mud so we sat in odd positions, cramped and wet from a light rain. By day the odd shell burst around, so the colonel, with great wisdom, forbade anyone moving around the tanks to run. We plodded from place to place or tank to tank rather as the infantry had plodded through the shelled village, dogged, unhurrying, and unhappy about where the next shell might land. My two frightened men got worse and once when some Jerry planes came over low I trod on the operator when I was trying to follow their flight with the machine gun.

Fortunately our rest was short and again I was detailed

for liaison, but this time to a Canadian brigade. This entailed going to a divisional conference where the most junior rank would be a captain. As a corporal this posed problems but I put on a leather jacket which covered up the giveaway stripes and lack of pips.

I was flattered by the job and impressed by the calm and detailed way in which we were briefed, though I was always suspicious of plans that had to dovetail too well. I never met a battle which went according to plan and in which there was not some time when contact was lost.

When the regiment moved, my troop made its separate way to our assignment with the Canadians, who greeted me most casually and pleasantly and invited me into the mess. I didn't mind them knowing that I was a corporal but suspected that my task would be all the harder if they did, so I declined as politely as I could.

We, the crews of the two tanks, ate pleasantly on a stretch of short, dry grass beside the brigade HQ and lay in the evening sun smoking and luxuriating in being able to relax and stretch at one and the same time. In spite of the odd shelling I opted to sleep beside the tank on the luxury of the dry ground, for I felt that the following day might well be trying and the attack was due to start before dawn.

I lay marvelling at my infinite luxury as I smoked a last pipe. Putting pipe, tobacco and matches into my boot for safe keeping, I drifted off, as contented a man as ever there was. I awoke to loud bangs and a thump in the back. I pulled my blankets closer and buried my head. Was it a piece of mud thrown up by a bomb? There were aircraft overhead. As I dozed again amid the bedlam of ack-ack fire and bomb bursts safe in the warmth of my blankets, a warm trickle ran down my back, paused, and then raced down the hollow of my spine. I passed a hand along and found a wet patch on my shoulder, then a hole the size of the end of my finger; no pain.

I told Chalky that I was going to a dressing station, and made my way from guarded light to guarded light until I found a three-ton truck being used to treat casualties. A man was brought in with severe cordite burns to his hands, and I stood humbly aside, imagining his agony. The orderly patched me up with a dressing and I made my way back to the tanks. We made some tea on a petrol stove and passed the rest of the night dozing and smoking.

I arrived at the control point before the day had shown its face, and was met by two operators sheltering in a trench covered with a very perforated ground sheet, glumly facing a ruined wireless set.

The day came but there was still no communication and I sat waiting to announce the reaching of a crucial point whereupon the tanks could begin their task. The sun came up and what I took to be the brigade major sat in his van reading *Esquire* and drinking tea.

Slowly messages began to come back—the usual hold-ups, counter-attacks. But now things were moving and my map had a scrawl of coloured chinagraph lines on it. Intelligence officers coming in from other units, seeing me, were asking and receiving a briefing on the position. I was too tired and stiff by now to care, and I was pretty sure that I had as much information as any one else.

The tanks made their way forward and there was jubilant report of successes. I was happy; they certainly deserved the successes. Then the German Tigers joined in and there were swift reports of tanks brewing and calls for the doctor. Frustration set in. With the guns we had, it was almost impossible to winkle out the heavily-armoured and magnificently-gunned German tanks.

Rocket-firing Typhoons were our only recourse and this was not the best thing for the morale of the tank crews. Smoke shells were fired to identify the German positions and they, with great presence of mind, fired them back at our positions, giving the impartial Typhoon a field day. The Canadians were aggrieved at one of their tanks being knocked out and I had a tedious tangle to untie, especially as no one wanted to listen.

By three-thirty I had had enough. The attack had bogged down, minds were numb and I was feeling actively sick. I took my small pack, said goodbye to my crew and Chalky, and made my way back to a forward dressing station. From there it was a line of stations, M and B tablets and tetanus jabs.

In the early evening a van load of us arrived at a field hospital, gentle in the green Normandy fields. They made us welcome and we lay in the evening sun smoking and drinking tea. Their kindness and gentleness almost reduced me to tears. A lethargy stole over me. For the moment I could do nothing, was expected to do nothing, and even my inner mind was prepared to let me rest. There was nothing here for me to learn, nothing to test my courage.

Lying in a real bed in a great tented ward, the lights very dim, the air warm and muggy, I slept leadenly but not deeply. Quiet figures were working among the innumerable beds, turning back the covers, looking, probing gently, making notes, unceasingly kind and gentle. I hardly woke as they looked at my shoulder. By ambulance to the beach-head, a DUKW amphibious truck out to a hospital ship and the magic was gone, only the staleness and pent-up feelings remained.

This was part of Britain and I preferred the army. By ambulance train, stark white and simple but kind, to hospital and real beds and stuffy air and routine, but a bath. Two days and then dressed and back in the train. Where to? To Falkirk! All wounded would be treated as near home as possible, but I suppose that as walking wounded we could reasonably go further afield. I slept on the floor of the train. Early in the morning we left the train and were met by a women's organisation giving out smiles and packets of cigarettes. Anger welled inside me and yet I was ashamed not to be able to thank them for their cold comfortless efforts to bring some humanity to us. To a long immaculate ward, an immaculate bed and a dragon of a sister.

Chapter 10

WE WERE BUSTLED into bed and pyjamaed. Clean, and ordered to match the long gleaming ward and the brisk nurses, we were left in no doubt that there we would lie, in the proper posture, until we had been inspected by the doctor.

Next to me was Frank from B squadron, with a grin hidden just below the surface and a monstrous soiled bandage round his head. He told me his story. His tank was one of those I had heard reported as knocked out. The lap gunner was killed and the driver seriously wounded, while Frank with his usual luck was nicked on the forehead by a piece of flying metal. They were taken back to HQ where the driver was laid out to await the ambulance and given morphia. Some enthusiast wrapped a vast bandage round Frank's head, which had a liberal coating of blood. When the ambulance arrived, Frank was at the front end of the stretcher on which they bore the wounded driver, so he entered the ambulance first. The wounded man being deposited satisfactorily, the orderly, who took his job seriously, pushed Frank on to a seat and swung the doors shut. By then he was in the sausage machine which was working with super efficiency, so that it was not until the doctor made his rounds, and the long bandage unwrapped, that Frank's scratch was uncovered to medical scrutiny. Within the hour he was dressed again and was off with a leave pass for fourteen days in his pocket and a grin no longer

153

hidden.

I was told that the shrapnel in my shoulder would work out of its own accord and there would be no need of surgery. I appreciated the thorough and straightforward way the doctor dealt with us and the way he talked about his ideas on treatment. He really did believe that it was my shoulder and it mattered to me how it was dealt with. In consequence of this I was soon up and about and undergoing physiotherapy, or at least a very sound and practical way of applying it. Presumably the best way to work a piece of shrapnel out of your shoulder is to use it rhythmically, and what better way than to polish the huge gleaming wood floor with a heavy bumper, to sweep the curtains, to dust the walls, even to carry the beds from side to side when cleaning. It certainly was no great hardship and it worked wonderfully well.

Most of us walking wounded woke at dawn, washed, breakfasted and then set to work in the ward. All twenty beds were carried from their position along one wall over to the other side of the ward. If there was an occupant who was confined to his bed he went along too. Once one side was clear the walls were swept, the windows cleaned, the curtains brushed, and then came the serious business of polishing the floor and burnishing it until it gleamed. Carry all the beds back again and repeat the performance on the other side. Once this was done came the *pièce de résistance*; the end beds were correctly stationed so that they were exactly square with the wall and exactly the right distance from it. Then a piece of string was stretched between the two and all the other beds were lined up, exactly in line and exactly equidistant. Lockers were placed correctly between the beds, covers were smoothed down and all was ready for the big moment when the matron and doctor could advance down one side of the ward and back up the other. Until their appearance we had to move delicately in case the beauty of the ward should be in any way disturbed. Once the doctor had made his rounds we might relax by sitting on a wooden chair, but the beds were sacrosanct and must only be used for sleeping.

On top of this, and in addition to the odd washing up, we suffered the further indignity of having to wear the most hideous uniform yet devised for man. A bright blue jacket and trouser suit made out of some sort of blanket material, quite shapeless and laundered into all sorts of weird creases, a violent red tie, a shapeless white thing called a shirt, and our old friends, army boots. We felt like a mixture of a pantomime comedian and a pauper in an institute. I have always felt that there was an underlying plan behind all this degradation inflicted in military hospitals. No one but those physically unable to leave would stay one minute longer than was absolutely necessary, unless he were a scrounger, in which case he was usually not much good at the front.

Wearing this dreadful garb, I used to make my way into Edinburgh to a friend of my mother's, who by her vivacity and intellectual capacity took me out of myself and made me forget that I was dressed like some sort of clown who was employed totally on domestic chores. I spent many happy afternoons with her and with the people of Edinburgh. With them I rejoiced at the advance of the allies out of Normandy, and thought with some envy of the regiment at last freed from close fighting and now moving across the north of Europe.

One day, on visiting the doctor, I found him surrounded by medical students and found myself exhibit A in his lecture. They all studied my shoulder. He then took a probe, put it in the hole until it scratched on the shrapnel, and commanded them to listen. I wondered if this was really to my advantage, but as it didn't hurt and it might do them some good, I felt that I had better bear it with fortitude. A few days later he pulled the metal out and presented me with it—a souvenir of the virtues of floor polishing. It wasn't many days before the hole had healed enough for me to leave my hideous blue uniform and these quiet serious people who were busy making us whole again. I said my goodbyes and made my way down to Cumberland, where my people were staying, and whither Joan was making her way from the south of England.

We spent a delicious fortnight in an old farmhouse standing on its own, guarded by a gnarled windswept old tree, surrounded by short sheep, cropped grass, and a drystone wall. To be with my own people was balm; to be with Joan was joy. I am not a city lover and by this time all towns were pretty tawdry. However, here in this simple and enduring landscape with its quiet life, ordered by the dictates of the climate and the relief of the land, I found complete peace and rest. I knew now that though I was frightened in battle it was something I could manage quite satisfactorily. As for further tests to come, they could wait for the moment.

We walked over the hills and across the moors, watched the sheep dogs working to the whistle on the opposite hillside, wandered down to the farm further down the valley to collect milk and chat in the peace of the evening. Down below in the valley was a small country pub for a quiet half pint, and once we went into the market town to shop with the sturdy cheerful farming community who made up the area.

The time passed in a dream but was endless. I had no more burdens to carry, I believed in a God, so what terrors did death hold except the pain of dying? On top of this I had someone of my own to love and cherish, someone who had made the prospect of coming home at the end of it all an attraction, and without whom it would have been just as easy to stick my head out too far one day in sheer depression at the unending prospect.

I made my way to Catterick, or Hades or the abode of the dead, whichever you prefer, and reported myself as fit and well and ready to return to my unit. This impressed no one, because they ran a sausage machine and I had to make a full circuit of this before more could be done. In fact it might land me in Europe once again— it might even return me to my unit—but on the other hand I might end up in the Seychelles tending a herd of ducks. In this vast, straggling camp were men from all the branches of the armoured corps coming and going to all theatres of war, nearly all in transit.

While a draft was being made up we spent much time up on the gorgeous moors walking and map reading, which was a delight. Once we were sent to escort a train-load of German prisoners to Liverpool, whence they were bound for Canada. We were injected, kitted out again and documented, and we sat about and waited and wondered at some of the gorgeous insignia worn by cavalry men discarded by their units when they were mechanised. I was irked that so many sergeants seemed to inhabit this backwater when many people such as myself were waiting for promotion. Obviously the army did not believe in the rate for the job.

After some two weeks a draft of us left Darlington station in transit for Europe, via a camp outside Aldershot. My shoulder was bleeding from the web equipment which I was wearing and I had to stand on one foot all the way to London, but I was eager to get back and help to finish the beastly job.

On arrival in Aldershot we enquired of transport to take us to our transit camp, but found that it had moved across the channel two days before. So we planted ourselves on another transit unit, who, with great presence of mind, sent us on thirty-six hours' leave while they sorted out the mess. Joan came up to London and we were happy and peaceful together, and then I returned to camp.

The weather was gorgeous and my companions congenial, so life was good. We were standing idly beside the road, hands in pockets, berets on the backs of our heads, dreaming, when to our astonishment what should come round the corner but a unit on the move with a band in the lead. We stood, gazing entranced at this splendid sight, until a roar from a proud and jaunty figure leading the troops made us aware of military matters, such as standing at attention and saluting.

We were shipped off from Aldershot to a camp near Cuckfield in Sussex. We thoroughly enjoyed our train ride, and the fact that it was a camp for Royal Engineers who sent us on thirty-six hours' leave while they found out what to do with us. This time I was near Joan and merely made my way to her home. On our return we were sent back to Aldershot to a unit which could actually deal with us once the details had been settled. Once again we went on thirty-six hours' leave to London, but by this time Joan's employers were getting rather weary. Whether our new camp pulled any strings or whether the sausage machine had got to the end of its gyrations I do not know, but on our return we found a draft made up and we were soon on our way.

Back again to the south coast where we were loaded on to an infantry landing ship, but a very much better version than the type seen back in Homs in North Africa, for in place of hard wooden seats this one had three-tier bunks. Though there was precious little room above, you at least could while away the voyage in comfortable sleep.

We took our rations with us in the shape of compo boxes, which contained a complete set of rations for fourteen men for one day. As we boarded the ship in the evening we had one meal, shared out the cigarettes and chocolate, and then slept, arriving in France with the sun the next morning.

A square harbour surrounded by cobbled roads and houses; Cinzano and Dubonnet and marbled tables. We weren't allowed to linger but were carted away in trucks to a transit camp outside the town, where we ate, were numbered, and eventually shipped off to a railway siding. Here we were loaded into the traditional 'huit chevaux ou quarante hommes' in about that proportion, and after some delay steamed off into the unknown.

Early on in our wanderings three of us from the same division had teamed up, and as each had been in charge of a ration box we had ample supplies in our van and also some 'tommy cookers' on which we could cook. On top of this we had all spent some time at this army business whilst most of our unfortunate party were reinforcements going out for the first time and were not really prepared for the eccentricities in the life of a reinforcement.

We stretched as best we could on the floor of the van— a jumble of equipment, legs and hard boards. The sun shone in through the doors which we had slid open and it was restful to lie there smoking while someone else did all the work and had all the headaches.

Some time in the early afternoon we stopped beside a cookhouse and collected a hot tin of meat and vegetables and a mug of tea, and there was the opportunity to attend to the calls of nature without hanging out of the doors. Evening drew on and still we ambled on. We made tea, spread a blanket and dozed quietly through the night. Dawn found us parked in a siding in Amiens, stiff and hungry. Men were streaming out of the wagons over the tracks and away into the town to eat, drink and stretch. Some directed their attention to trucks loaded with rations, but we dealt rather summarily with them. When it became obvious that our journey could not be resumed until the wanderers had been rounded up, we too left the station for a stretch and a wander round.

In the middle of the day we were moving again but the sky was grey and we were bored with the whole business. For a while the train stopped beside a potato field and soon there was a considerable gathering in the field harvesting some sort of a meal. Roars of protest from the officer in charge had them back in the train and we wended our sluggish way.

That night we finished the rations, for with a truck load to feed our ample supplies became meagre, and it was with considerable graitification that we were unloaded somewhere in Belgium at noon the next day and taken to a Royal Artillery transit camp near Brussels. Here we were fed and given a tent to sleep in. As it grew dusk we wandered out of the camp and found ourselves a warm bright café beside the road and drank beer, talked and savoured the strange and conflicting smells. Autumn was obviously on us as we walked back to the camp and curled gratefully in our blankets.

But still the gods were not propitiated for in the middle of the night we were aroused, loaded into trucks, and borne off. After what seemed an endless journey, we drove through the large double gates of a barracks on to the parade ground and shuffled our way into a medieval building where we found bunks for the night.

By then it must have been nearly three in the morning, so that when reveille sounded at six we felt that we could well lie in, until an ear-splitting roar announced the arrival of the sergeant-major. From then on for the rest of the day we seemed to be fleeing in front of him on some duty or another and scarcely had time to view this strange edifice.

I had seen barrack buildings before, especially in France and Belgium, or rather I had seen the high walls round them and the sentries at the gate. It was quite a new experience to be inside; not unlike a gaol, I imagine. Much to our relief we were loaded up the next morning and carried away in the back of three-ton trucks to our divisional reinforcement camp.

A typical flat Belgium landscape, heavy with trees, in places their leaves turning colour and falling in a cold gusty wind; the sky overcast; pools of damp leaves beside the road; fields heavy with unharvested beet or bare with the stubble of a corn harvest. Tram lines winding down the roadsides, hedgeless fields and neat houses tucked away in the shelter of their poplars. The bridges over the canals were mostly blown, and at each one there was a diversion. Often there was a knocked-out gun or tank—a harsh reminder to us of our easy life.

The camp was drab, part tented, part in farm buildings; our reception bored and indifferent. We were documented and signed for, fed, given a space in which to sleep and left to our devices. The next day we were divided up. Those who belonged to no regiment were posted to one and departed in the back of a truck. Those of us belonging to regiments were put to some trivial work.

I had learnt my lesson in Africa, so the next day I did not report for work but got out on the road and hitched my way up to the unit, which fortunately was out of the line. I met UJ who said that they were short of NCOs and concurred to my suggestion that they send a DR to the camp to ask for me to be posted back at once. So I came back.

The unit was billeted in a small village and I found my cronies, or those who were left cooking an evening meal, beside their tanks outside a small cottage in which they were sleeping. The light of the day was going and the wind was cold. Across the brown fields I could see the harvesters picking potatoes from the ground. I watched a girl bending easily with knees straight, feet firmly in her clogs, picking potatoes from the ground.

I was still an outcast, without a tank and without a crew, but Trig and Goodie fed me from their rations and made me welcome. I went to bed that night subdued and sad with thoughts of the sunny days at home. When I woke I was back again. The job still had to be done and still I had not tested myself to the full.

Chapter 11

THE BRIEF PERIOD of melancholy soon passed. I was sent down to Bechelon with a crew to collect a tank, and with a tank I had a home. I had somewhere to keep my few possessions, a stove and brew tin, rations, water, a complete *raison d'être*. We drew, that being the right word, from the quartermaster, a beautiful new Stewart tank, complete with twin Cadillac engines and an automatic gearbox. The gun was the same old peashooter, but then we were essentially for reconnaissance and this tank was quite and reliable. We didn't manage to draw the torches and map case that came with the tank, but then the quartermaster had no doubt better uses for them than us. How else could he find his way to the local café at night? Thus equipped we returned and soon rendered ourselves into one unit ready for our return to the line. I was lucky to have a young cheerful crew and we grew to trust and admire each other as the weeks went by.

I found many strange faces and learned of the demise of many old friends, but there was still a hard core left, especially some of the regular sergeants, for whom I had a profound admiration. Not only were they very competent indeed but they had the most wonderful philosophy which allowed them to surmount the impossible with quiet calm and humour.

I drank rum and evaporated milk in a half track with Alf in the dark of the early night, and we gossiped easily about what had befallen the regiment during my absence. The colonel was new to me and so was G, my new troop officer. I found him easy to work with, competent, and willing to allow me to use what initiative I might have. I was lucky indeed.

So one morning we made our way up the line to do our stint, a very easy stint, true, and an ideal return. The Arnhem offensive had been at its climax while I lay in the sun in Sussex and now it was all past except for the empty places at family tables and some memories. For the moment the line was static and we were holding part of it by day and being relieved at night by the infantry.

G and I were parked either side of the main road to block that and keep a wary eye on either side. Though near, we were out of sight of each other, so my crew and I settled down to a peaceful day in the autumn sunshine outside a small farmhouse which lay beside the road. With one man in the turret and the guns loaded we took it in turns to loaf, cook, smoke, and perhaps more important, to savour the last vestiges of summer.

This perhaps is the glory of the autumn. There is a wistful recognition of the profligacy of summer and a treasuring of each remaining ray of sun. As the sun sank over this empty landscape we withdrew and made ourselves at home in the loft over the cowshed of a small farm. Here, over the warmth of our petrol stoves, we rested as our supper cooked, and soon we were lying down warm from the cool autumn night and lulled by the rhythmic munching from the cattle below.

With the dawn we were back again in position and I made it a habit to do a foot patrol on arrival, carrying a sten gun and bucket. The bucket was for mushrooms which grew in profusion in the fields around, and for any eggs from the neighbouring hen houses which might have been left by any German patrol from the night before.

I did consider putting a booby trap in one but felt that this could become a two-way business. We found a lump of fat bacon hanging in an outhouse of the farm and feasted on bacon, fresh eggs and mushrooms, and thus fortified passed one more golden day to return to the warmth and rhythm of our bedroom.

On the third day I ventured further on foot during the afternoon and made my way to the crossroads where lay three of our tanks, knocked out by bazookas just before I rejoined the unit. This we took to be the dividing line. On one side of the crossroads were houses and I made my way through them to get a good view of the German side. Very quietly I went, trying to avoid any untoward noise which might alert a Jerry, but was frustrated in this by the attentions of the animals left behind when the houses were evacuated.

So I led the way, creeping stealthily along, followed by a couple of cats which mewed and purred alternately, a few dogs which were apt to bark excitedly, and even a pig emitting grunts. After a few moments the humour of the thing overtook me and I gave up and stroked the animals. Anything more absurd than this man creeping stealthily, steely-eyed, wary of a sudden Indian attack, followed by this motley array of lonely animals, was hard to imagine. They completely ignored my shushes, terrified me by suddenly rubbing against my legs and behaved as if they had no idea of the seriousness of the situation. I made my way back, inspected the knocked-out tanks, the body of a dead civilian lying in the road, mounted a bicycle and rode back down the road in bravado.

On the fourth day I visited the animals again and received a rapturous reception, particularly as I took some food with me. The day was uneventful, except for a horse and cart which arrived to collect a vast pig from the farm. This was loaded up and driven off, but such was the weight of the pig that the horse's legs barely touched the ground.

Again the fifth day was golden, except for the lap gunner who hated mushrooms and was having them three times a day. That afternoon we killed a hare to eat when we came out of the line on the morrow. During our perambulations we found a minute pig buried in the ground with just its snout showing, and took it back to the farm where we rested at night. Just to stir things up, before we withdrew that night, G fired a few rounds of HE through his gun at maximum elevation, and received a full return which kept our heads down for some time.

The four days out went in a flash and we were back to our post, but this time it was suggested that we might be a little more aggressive, so the first afternoon G's tank and mine made a gallant charge at what we considered to be the German line and were rewarded by an outburst of firing and mortar shells, which had no visible effect. Having effectively stirred the pot, we withdrew to cook our supper in peace before withdrawing for the night.

On the next afternoon I made my way down to the crossroads, skirted round the knocked-out tanks, and gained the far side of the road without attracting the attention of my four-legged friends. I had no particular plan but felt that I should probe a little further to find where the Germans were.

I made my way down a hedgerow. I saw nothing and stopped once or twice to consider my position. Once some shells flew gently overhead and I threw myself to the ground, although it was obvious that they were far away. My feet took me on for the best part of a mile when I approached a farm house. Around the edge of the farmyard were defensive positions which were obviously abandoned and littered with soggy German field post cards. Everything was still and deserted so I made my way into the farmyard and from there into the cow shed which was joined to the house. Some cows were ruminating quietly and gazed with unblinking eyes as I entered.

From the shed was a door into the house. I opened it quietly and there neatly beside the wall was a pair of jackboots. I tried them for size but they were too small. Down the passage and through a door on the right. Here was a litter of military occupation: pieces of equipment, a couple of bazookas, a sergeant-major's tunic, some hair clippers which I pocketed because we were in need of them. I went out and crossed to a room on the other side of the passage; nothing. Back into the passage and towards the back door, I heard an inner door open and flattened myself against the wall and cocked the sten gun silently and steadily.

I looked at my hands and they were quite steady. I examined my mind and was surprised to find it calm and quite unafraid. I interrogated myself on why I was there and the only answer was that my feet must have taken me. I was enchanted.

Through the door came a blond German soldier in shirt and stockinged feet, obviously fresh from his bed. He stared foolishly, rooted to the spot. I, too, stood rooted to the spot, because while I was analysing my mind, it would perhaps have been better if I had thought out some plan of action. If only I knew the German for 'hands up', we could perhaps make our way back to our lines. Suddenly he jumped for the door and swung it to; he was a good soldier. I fired low down at stomach height through the thin door panel and there was a terror-stricken high-pitched groan. Then the sten gun jammed.

I turned and ran, my boots clashing on the tiled floor of the passage. The cows flicked me a glance as I fled through and I was into the farmyard, past the slit trenches, down the hedgerow and on my way home. After half a mile I stopped, gasping for breath. I settled into a dry piece of ditch and rested; all was quiet and uneventful.

I walked slowly back and was given an ecstatic greeting by the cats, the dog and the pig. UJ was beside the tank when I returned and I told my tale and showed my booty. I don't know if he believed me.

That night on guard I was really frightened as reaction set in. I wondered why I had gone and what I had gone for and it was all quite plain. I thought back to what had been a recurring question: what did it feel like when you were face to face? All through my army career I had had to fight my way up to the fighting line and almost continuously I had been baulked. Deep down within me this urge to know had carried me forward, and this afternoon it had taken my unwitting body to find out. It hadn't taken the hero of the novel but plain ordinary me. I had stood in the passage quietly, calmly, had cocked the gun without a tremor. Only at the last moment had I abandoned my heroic part. At last I knew what I had searched for. It was comforting to rejoin my blankets and to doze off to the gentle sounds of the manger.

Another day of peace and we returned for the last morning ready to be relieved by the infantry. All the crews had their eye on some hapless hare or chicken which they were reckoning to take with them when we withdrew, so that it was not surprising that there was a report of small arms fire all along our sector of the front the next morning. Have no fear, it was merely the recce troop shooting its supper.

After my experience with a sten I decided to acquire a German machine pistol at the first opportunity as being both better and more reliable. I also had a German sniping rifle with a beautiful telescopic sight. My trousers were kept up with German belt and I also ate off a fine German enamel plate. It would almost be fair to say that I was almost a Germophile.

We came back out of the line and watched the infantry moving in, ready for the next advance forward. This was a clearing operation in which we were to be involved, and was aimed at our area of Holland as far as the river Maas. Infantry were now scarce and a lot of the work which we had to do could reasonably have been done better and more easily by them. With a maze of canals and dykes we were often groping around for a way forward and when we found one, it was often a soft tree-lined track with a dyke either side, so once on it you were committed to moving forward, praying quietly that there wasn't an anti-tank gun at the other end. Over the mantelpiece at home I have a painting of just such a track as a reminder of the many prayers I said.

The Germans, though not standing fast, gave ground reluctantly, and had developed their technique of bazooka teams to a fine art. Their bazooka was a simple weapon consisting of a hollow charge bomb capable of penetrating a tank, which was fired with a rocket charge. The rocket was housed in a thin metal tube with the bomb at the end and consequently was easy to carry and very easy to fire. A well-concealed infantryman could wait quite happily for a tank which, if not covered in the rear by another one, was a sitting duck.

The first day of this operation I spent peacefully guarding a bit of the flank. We were surrounded by woods and apart from shells cruising high overhead we were relaxed and content. On one of my perambulations I came across a dead German in a hedgerow and was about to walk down into the ditch to get his pay-book, when I hesitated, looked down carefully, and saw the corner of one of their little Schoe mines which they spread around liberally. They were very difficult to detect and, though small, were very well able to destroy a foot, the philosophy being that a footless man was a greater burden to a country than a dead one. I got to the body by a different route and found that he had crawled on to one of his own mines. Inside the pay book was five pounds in guilders which I pocketed.

The unit began its advance the next day, and as night came down we were strung out down the road playing hide-and-seek with bazooka teams. We passed a burning farmhouse whose occupants cheered us and waved one hand while throwing buckets of water on to the fire with the other. This was a heroism that made us all feel very small and insignificant and drove us on inexorably to show more courage and thrust.

One village after another was cleared and more often than not we found a billet for the night in the simple houses. If we were early enough we would pool our rations with the household, which was no doubt a great help to them, for meat was almost unknown, being all commandeered for the Reich. To us it was a pleasure to be able to sit down and eat pleasantly. Somewhere in this week I had a birthday, but it went unremembered and only afterwards when writing home did I realise that I was 27 and had spent the last five years having a war.

We were making our way towards Ousterhout, which was substantially our final objective, when we met the usual blown bridge and blocked track difficulty, and I was sent out on the flank to look for an alternative route over a canal. Finding my bridge intact I radioed back and was met by the infuriating query 'Was I sure?' 'I'm parked on the bridge now!' The colonel was out in his scout car, so I sat on the bridge for some time until it was accepted as being there and then only when UJ came to have a look. I often wondered why I bothered to stick my neck out and why I didn't find a nice quiet corner and brew some tea.

The tanks came down the road and started towards the

town, but with infinite caution, so I took off down the road. With us we had a Dutch resistance fighter who walked round the first corner to see if all was clear and was met with a violent burst from a sub machine gun. I looked for a riddled body, but he came back unharmed, if a little breathless. G stuck to the road and I swung off to the left and set off across the field. Immediately in front of us was a twenty millimetre machine gun, which was fairly innocuous against our armour, so we charged it and threw a smoke grenade into the pit, effectively clearing out the crew who were then trapped in the open.

The heavies were still firing at some infantry dug into the woods on their front, so we just kept going. My fear gauge was registering nil and I was feeling thoroughly aggressive. Swiftly we came to our objective and I reported this and asked for the next move, but was directed to do something useful. This I appreciated but wanted to know in which direction I could be most useful. Nothing.

There were Germans running in many directions, so we helped them on their way with the browning machine gun. Some ran into a house, so we put a few rounds of HE in after them. Across a field to our front three Germans took off on foot with about 150 yards start and we took off after them, firing as we went. The bullets were cutting an arc between the ground in front of the tank and the sky as we rocked over the rough ground with the gunner desperately trying to keep the gun level. We were now all reduced to the level of primaeval animals running their quarry down, so thin is our veneer of civilisation. I was baying over the intercom, the gunner was drooling, and the driver was beating his steed for the utmost effort. One of the Jerries fell and the other two stopped.

We came up to them and once they had raised their

hands I dismounted, and while the gunner held the machine pistol, I went forward. A very obnoxious and aggressive squat German officer began to tell me what to do about the prisoner who had been shot through the thigh and was in real pain. I could readily have shot him, but forbore. Round his neck he had a beautiful pair of Zeiss glasses, which I removed and used from then onwards. We lifted the wounded man on to the back of the tank and marched the other two back to the road and left the three of them in the care of the troops coming up.

G and I made our way into the centre of the town and out the other side to see that all was clear. There I was left to keep watch. By then the centre of the town was jubilation and rejoicing. We sat on our crossroads for the rest of the afternoon, no doubt forgotten, until with the coming of darkness I rang up and asked for orders and was told to return. We were billeted in the house of the police chief in the centre of the town, which was very comfortable, and we were made much of.

The Germans still shelled the town occasionally— with little effect—and for the next week I went daily out to the north towards the Mass and watched an area bounded on our front by a canal and on our left by a canal whose far bank was still held by Jerry. Living out there in a big barge was a Dutch family and we spent the greater part of our time on board the barge with them. At intervals we came out and shot at any German heads which we could see, but they were decent and left us in peace. Time went swiftly with an accordion and a small dog, the family's tales of the waterways of Europe, and our return in the evening to a gracious house and some comfort.

I was promoted to sergeant and the daughters of our billet vied for the honour of sewing on the new stripes. Then quite out of the blue I was told that I could go down to Brussels for four days' leave. This came as quite a shock because I had been back such a short time and didn't even know that there was such a thing as leave. It was gay, and sleeping in a bed and having a bath were luxuries which I enjoyed to the full. Beer was plentiful and there were lots of pretty girls to look at and French cosmetics to buy for Joan, but I wasn't refreshed, only rested.

Our area was now clear and settled, and we moved south as the winter came on, into a position of reserve. It was a bitter cold day when we moved, with a strong wind and driving rain, so that I travelled with my umbrella up. We pulled off the road at midday for a break and a meal, and were sitting round a fire drinking hot tea and thawing out when a new young officer arrived enquiring if the maintenance had been done on the tanks. I was rather blunt and pointed out that in my troop we were doing some maintenance on the crews, who were much harder to replace than the tanks.

We were well billeted through a long straggling village, and considering the lot of many of the troops, we were living in luxury, but I felt fractious and discontented. In fact I had had enough, and though I could manage the fighting end of the business, living the life of a serf had grown irksome, and I found it all very hard to bear.

My tank was in first-class order and we kept it that way. My crew were good and we could work well together, and I was always happy to learn the arts of fighting and killing. But I was no longer prepared to take all the saluting and ordering and dressing up seriously, and as we did practically nothing for five weeks I became thoroughly discontented. I desperately wanted to see the end of the war; this was now the one driving urge which kept me going.

There were good sides to our life. My crew and I lived in the house of a cobbler, sleeping at night in the living room, which housed a shiny metal stove on which the food was cooked. We handed over our rations, the family added what they could, and we all ate together. In the evenings we would sit round the stove and gossip and doze, waiting until we could roll our blankets out and sleep. Alf, with great presence of mind, was billeted in the local café and was his usual even, composed self. Goodie was billeted in a small farmhouse which boasted an earth closet in a building between two pig sties, so it was possible to sit in state and converse with the pigs or consider their condition at the same time. I was rather shattered one day when the farmer's daughter came in to feed the pigs. She was quite unabashed, so we passed pleasantries, and I waited until she had left before rising.

I spent a few days on a camouflage course, which I found very interesting, and could have been some use. We discussed the question of camouflage in the snow and learned with chagrin that there was not enough equipment to go round. Apart from this we went through the routine of doing things without ever doing anything properly. The whole episode became like a very badly-prepared lesson. The students became fractious and ill-disciplined and authority began to wield the stick. A halfhearted and petty purge was started, which because it wasn't thought out or carried through properly made us all more cynical. In the middle of it all we had to devote the better part of a day looking for a jeep which two fairly senior officers had lost when drunk.

Fortunately we moved, leaving our tanks behind, and went up the line to help the poor overworked infantry. Our task was to take over some of the night and patrol work from them, and give them a chance to rest a little. Unfortunately the area given to the division to hold was then in the possession of a Guards brigade, so that no sooner had we arrived than I found myself marching a squad up and down the muddy street of a village. This was really more than I could bear. I marched my lot away in the mist until out of sight and fell them out, while I stood like an imbecile and shouted orders for the sake of authority down the road.

The next day I went sick with a sore toe. This meant missing a night patrol, but anything was preferable to the pathetic efforts on the village street. Our job was to be really efficient in the fighting of the tanks, and this we should have worked at. In the middle of this pantomime the Germans made their thrust in the Ardennes, and we were returned to our tanks again and moved to a small village just short of the German border.

Life was immediately better; there was some urgency in the air. We spent quite a considerable time moving round the area to make sure that we knew the topography. In a deserted German village we found large supplies of bottled vegetables and fruit, which we found excellent, although we were warned that they might be doctored with arsenic. On one trip we brought back a gas cooker for the farmhouse in which we were billeted. This was a poor farm and we watched with fasination as the family threshed their corn with flails and then winnowed it.

I knew by now that I had had enough war. I applied for a commission, feeling that this would get me away for some time and also give me something to learn and struggle for. In its own right this was successful, for I had to appear cheerful and efficient, which was an incentive. The purge went on in its silly way. One day it was decided that there would be an inspection of the guns, so we stripped the three browning machine guns and the breech of the 37 mm to their smallest component part and then mixed them up in a great big bowl and offered them for inspection, knowing very well that the inspectors would have been very hard pushed to assemble them again.

It was nearly Christmas and the snow came with a hard frost which covered the dykes with thick ice and the bare land with a thick white coating. We huddled round the stove in our billet when we could find fuel. At night as we lay on the floor we were cold with howling draughts, but how much better off than the wretched infantry stuck in a narrow slit trench in a forward post. On guard at night my feet froze and I thought with longing of the felt boots of our Russian allies.

There was the usual effort to make Christmas jolly, but it only enhanced the barrenness of our position. We had some drink supplied and strict orders not to get drunk. This I resented as it seemed incredible that any responsible and experienced soldier would leave himself wide open to attack at such a time and with such an enemy. What was my fury to find that the guard had picked up one of our officers dead drunk and lying in the village street. Had I been guard commander, I should have thrown him on one of the many dung heaps and left him there.

In the event Christmas passed happily enough for us, though the Luftwaffe took the opportunity to strike at celebrating air bases. This they repeated on 1 January, and we all had a field day as they came back from the raid, low in fuel and out of ammunition. It was like a rather good pheasant shoot with the birds coming in low and fast as they made their way home. Our light machine guns no doubt did little good except excite us, though they did sever a power line that fell to the ground and sparked enormously until it went dead.

Early in January we were briefed for a new attack northwards to clear another salient up to the river Roer. It was certainly an ambitious plan, demanding very close co-ordination between many branches and excellent timing. It also meant frozen ground in order to get over some of the waterlogged areas. We said our farewells to these hospitable people who had shared their homes with us without a grumble, people who were on their way to mass in the morning as we stood-to just before the dawn. And we said goodbye to the children who helped our depleted egos by treating us as all-conquering heroes.

We moved off on ice-covered roads and in a thick fog which held up the attack and gave us time to whitewash our tanks as some sort of camouflage. As darkness fell we were lined down the road waiting. Our new young officer came down the line with orders that we were not to brew up, but as I was parked beside a signals section who were busily boiling a large billy of water, I felt that I was hardly brewing up when I made some tea. Laced with rum it got us through the first part of a very cold night, sitting cramped in the ice-cold tanks. I had taken the precaution of bringing a sack of straw in which I could keep my feet, but by the morning I didn't know that I had any.

With the daylight came a thaw which, though slight, turned the tracks to quagmires and made everyone's task the harder. Slowly we made our way forward, but the main advance down the centre got bogged down and we were swung round to the side behind the infantry. All through the late afternoon we sat near a stream which the engineers and Pioneer corps were trying to bridge under constant mortar and shell fire. I watched the bursting shells and realised that though most fears had left me, this I hated.

As darkness came we made our way over the stream and spent the night in a wilderness of mud and dereliction beside a knocked-out ambulance that had got through before the ground thawed. I carried the brew can over to a burning haystack and, using a long pole, boiled it and made tea to see us through another cold night. We huddled in the tank and woke at intervals, passed the rum bottle round, and fell asleep immediately as the hot spirit spread through our veins. Half an hour later we woke and took another sparing drink.

Morning saw us on the move into the village which the infantry had cleared during the night. G and I were sent out to the east to cut the road north of the main advance, which was expected through during the day. As we made our way down the road I pulled off to the left and went across country out on the flank.

There were signs of hurried German evacuation. We came to a crossroads on the main road, tree-lined and pleasant in summer, but now bare and harsh. I stopped my tank beneath the trees to view the village the other side. Towards us walked two German soldiers, shrugging on their equipment as they walked. With our guns cocked we watched fascinated as they drew nearer and nearer. They stopped horror-stricken, turned and fled. Mac unleashed the tank and we took off after them firing madly, swerved through a farmyard and chased the fleeing grey figures out of the far end of the village. We came back to the farmyard, where there were two dead Germans flat on the discoloured snow.

Inside a barn filled with hay was a narrow passage in which crouched the farmer's family, forcibly hiding ten Germans. These we put in an air raid shelter outside where they could do no harm, and could be guarded with a tommy gun quite effectively. On the upper floor of an open-ended barn overlooking the yard were three more Jerries with a spandau machine gun, which in more determined hands could have finished us all off. These joined their comrades in their cold, dank hole.

G and I took stock and found that we had Germans on three sides of us, but at that time they were in some confusion and we had the advantage of surprise, so we kept moving round quietly, popping out of openings and firing across the desolate white fields to give some idea of numbers and also to stop any ideas they might have of forming a bazooka party to stalk us.

UJ came down to view the scene and the prisoners were removed, which freed our hands. We saw a small horse-drawn convoy making its way to an adjoining village and started to shoot it up, but I hadn't any heart in this. Ridiculously, wounding the horses worried me. We watched German troops moving into defensive positions on the edge of the village. A white-clad figure crept surreptitiously into a small brick-built hen house, so we put an HE shell in after him.

Another light tank was sent down to probe out southwards towards the main advance, but it met an anti-tank gun and was brewed up, fortunately without casualties. The long day wore on and on, and no one came from the south, where the going was very difficult indeed. As dusk fell we pulled out of the village; an armour-piercing shell hissed past as we crossed the main road.

The billet was warm with crowded bodies and cooking stoves when we arrived, tired and bleary. I was not happy at having to make my way back to the village on the morrow, when Jerry would have had plenty of time to prepare a reception party. I boasted that night that I had not lost any member of my tank crew to date.

With the first streaks of light we were down the road again, but I had left my gunner behind because he was due to go on leave. This seemed an utter stupidity, but no doubt the pressures at home to bring the boys back on leave were too pressing. Its effect on fighting troops was not good, for how well will a man fight when he knows he is going on leave the next day? How good is a crew when it is arbitrarily changed at the last minute? After five years why not wait the last few months?

To my relief there was no reception committee for us.

Off to our left we watched another of our tanks, engaging an anti-tank gun sighted down the main road As the gunners rose to manoeuvre the gun around some ninety degrees, we could see the tracer spraying from his machine gun against the leaden sky. We sent over some HE to make up for the shot at us the night before. Somewhere a rifle was firing at us. I parked out in the open and was sitting on the turret using my field glasses when UJ arrived, asking what I was doing. He replied that it seemed a very dangerous position and left. I began to think about it and realised that I didn't mind any more. I was tired of the whole thing, utterly weary, and death held an end; if it came it came.

Through the falling snow I watched a magpie, white breasted and puffed up, hopping near a dead German, a corpse lying on its back tightly swathed in a superb dark-grey overcoat. On the corpse's breast the snow was falling and with the white face and dark round helmet here was a larger magpie. The infantry came in and began to probe through to the east and north. Quietly they made their way down the ice-covered road. A man fell and the patrol took cover at the side of a house. The ice around the figure turned red and two men ran swiftly out, seized an arm each and tobogganed the body back to safety.

I felt that I couldn't sit surrounded with armour plate while this went on. We joined the hunt for the Germans and flushed a man from his lair, who ran darting like a hare. We had him trapped flat on the ground while the machine gun hammered at him. As the belt ran out he jumped up and was away. Finally we located a strongpoint dug behind a haystack. We tried to set the stack on fire with tracer from the machine gun but to no avail. We moved round to the other side, hoping to take it in the rear, but I couldn't get out into the open because of an anti-tank gun. Instead we made our way up a privet hedge which brought us to the very edge of the stack.

A small infantryman came out from behind the hedge, laughing away the tension of a miraculous escape when he had almost walked into the strongpoint. Together we threw grenades over the stack, but they did not explode—perhaps we had used too much grease on the pin mechanism which had now frozen in the bitter weather. I decided to use the tank. We drew in our heads and using the periscopes made our way down the hedge, swung round the corner, and there before us was the stack with the edge of the slit trenth showing behind it. As I saw this I saw a grey square face below a grey soft field cap—and a bazooka. The explosion stopped us dead and the tank was full of flame; the engine was still.

I baled out before the next shell came, twisting round to get out quicker. With my back to the Germans I came out of the turret and all in a split second felt something pass through my arm at the elbow, realised it was a bullet and realised also that it had not hurt at all. I dropped down behind the tank, protected from the machine gun which had cut the side of my tank suit to ribbons and done so little damage. My gunner dropped down beside me. He was wounded in the soles of both feet and couldn't walk. I explained that it was a case of running to the next hedge. The machine gun in the tank fired a few bursts and the driver dropped down. He was bleeding from the nose, mouth, eyes and ears and had come up in huge bumps on his face, but was very brave and cool. The lap gunner was gone. I took hold of Mac and with the gunner we made a shambling run of it for the hedge. Once there help came, and a farmhouse and bandages and back to RHQ on a scout car. I walked up the street, black, burnt, arm in a sling, leg full of little pieces of tank and feeling calmly happy. Since then I have fought that one engagement ten thousand times and not lost the lap gunner.

Back through the mill of aid posts, where I was treated by a doctor whom I was at school with, and we gossiped briefly about mutual acquaintances. Finally, full of anti-tetanus, we reached a forward hospital, where again I found kindness and gentleness. A nurse cut Mac's tank suit to ribbons rather than unzip it and they got to work on him. I had a hole through the flesh of the elbow, which was neither very painful nor serious. I never saw Mac again, for we were separated and went back down different lines.

I arrived at a small clearing hospital, but had to be parked in an outside washhouse because the label fastened to the stretcher which bore my particulars had got lost. By midday I was admitted and lay on my stretcher and chatted to a nurse from Falmouth as she shaved me and cleaned my filthy face.

And back and back until at last a large base hospital at Louvaine, and military discipline and fatigues. With my right arm in a sling I was taken down to the basement kitchen and given a large tub of apples to core. Eventually I hit on the idea of laying them out on the stone floor and stabbing them with the corer held in my left hand. I certainly made a hole in them all, even if I didn't remove the core. Three dreadful weeks saw me out of the ghastly place, and the RSM at the transit camp in Brussels seemed a quiet genial fellow after the nurses in the base hospital.

I found the unit moved again and holding the line of the river under the command of the 9th American Army. I heard the gossip in the B and A echelons, chief of which was that the colonel's staff car had set out for France to buy brandy. Back with the recce troop I was forlorn again. The next day I was told to report to the colonel, who had UJ in attendance, and I was told that I had been recommended for a court martial for writing a letter home saying that I thought the colonel was a fool and the unit a shower. 'What had I to say?' I had very little to say. I was too flabbergasted and furious to say much to this smug-faced pair. Had I broken any security regulations I could have understood it. I had also been recommended for a commission and was to leave the regiment forthwith and go back to a selection board.

I left the regiment that very afternoon, without goodbyes. I was cold with fury. The war was over for me and nothing would have induced me to lift a finger, literally nothing. At selection board I was offered an immediate commission and a return to my unit. I managed to be sent back to Sandhurst.

On honeymoon in Bournemouth, Joan and I met G quite by chance, who told me that I had been recommended for the Military Medal, but of course bad conduct put paid to that. I would have liked it.

On VE day in Camberley I put a fistful of notes on the counter of the pub for everyone to drink to those who weren't coming back. With a general lack of understanding and the catch in my throat it was not a success.

Dhahran, Saudi Arabia.

Postscript

THERE WAS A general feeling in the armoured regiments that we were at a grave disadvantage with the Germans because their tanks had better armour and better guns.

The Imperial War Museum supplied me with details of armour and gun performance of the allied and German tanks and this partly bears out our feelings.

In the desert war prior to Knightsbridge and the retreat to Alamein the German Mark III and Mark IV tanks had their front plate armour of 62 mm and 60 mm respectively; the allied 2 pounder and 37 mm tank guns had a maximum penetration of 58 mm at 250 yards which often meant that the German tanks were only vulnerable in the turret, side and rear. At the same time their guns were heavier. The tale is even more daunting when it comes to anti-tank guns for the Allies had the 2 pounder (approx. 40 mm) while the Germans had the 37 mm, 50 mm, 75 mm and their very formidable 88 mm Anti-aircraft/Anti-tank gun; this is given as penetrating 83 mm of armour at 2000 yds. No wonder that in Bingo games the call was 'All the eights, 88, bale out'.

At El Alamein with the Grant and Sherman with their 75 mm guns and the 6 pounder anti-tank gun we had reasonable parity which continued to the end of the North African campaign.

So the war in Africa ended, we moved to Italy and then back to Britain in preparation for Normandy. There, our Cromwells carrying a 75 mm gun, were unable to penetrate the frontal armour of the German Panthers or Tigers, but could just penetrate that of the Mark III and IV at ranges under 1000 yards, which, in the thick Normandy bocage, was a normal range of engagement. However our 17-pounder Shermans, of which we had one in each troop, could penetrate the frontal armour of all their tanks at ranges up to 2000 yds and even over that, if they were lucky enough to get a hit at such long ranges. All the German tanks could penetrate the frontal armour of all our tanks at ranges up to 1500 yards, the Panthers and Tigers beyond that.

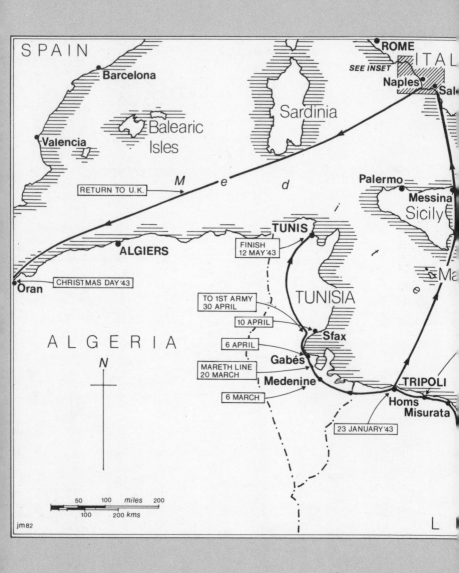

The travels of Peter Roach and the 8th Arm